ENGLISH CLASSICS — NEW SERIES

SELECTIONS FROM PIERS PLOWMAN

English Classics — New Series

★

SELECTIONS FROM PIERS PLOWMAN

EDITED

WITH AN INTRODUCTION AND NOTES

BY

COLIN WILCOCKSON, M.A.

Senior English Master, The Leys School, Cambridge

MACMILLAN

Melbourne · London · Toronto

ST MARTIN'S PRESS

New York

1965

MACMILLAN AND COMPANY LIMITED
St Martin's Street London WC 2
also Bombay Calcutta Madras Melbourne

THE MACMILLAN COMPANY OF CANADA LIMITED
70 Bond Street Toronto 2

ST MARTIN'S PRESS INC
175 Fifth Avenue New York 10010 NY

PRINTED IN GREAT BRITAIN

Contents

Acknowledgements

I wish to acknowledge my gratitude to the following:

For assistance in arranging the glossary: Mrs. S. W. Venables, and two former pupils, J. F. Dyball, now of Keble College, Oxford, and D. J. Rogers, now of Fitzwilliam House, Cambridge.

For help in checking the proofs: my colleague, Mr. M. F. Howard, and a former pupil, T. J. Bisseker, now of Jesus College, Cambridge.

For guidance on a number of philological points: Dr. P. A. M. Clemoes of Emmanuel College, Cambridge.

For help with the illustrations: Miss P. M. Giles, Librarian of the Fitzwilliam Museum; Mr. A. Halcrow, Assistant Librarian of Trinity College, Cambridge; Mr. W. G. Ingram; and Mr. J. Winny of Selwyn College, Cambridge.

Throughout the preparation of the edition, I have been indebted to the scholarly work of the late W. W. Skeat.

To all the above I am most grateful. Any errors that remain in the book are due entirely to myself.

I also wish to thank the following, who have kindly given permission for the use of copyright material: Messrs. Basil Blackwell & Mott, Ltd., for the extract from 'The Character of Piers Plowman Considered from the B Text', by Nevill Coghill, from *Medium Aevum*, vol. 2, 1933; Cambridge University Press, for the extract from *Preaching in Medieval England*, by G. R. Owst; Messrs. Jonathan Cape, Ltd., for the extract from *Man's Unconquerable Mind*, by R. W. Chambers; and The Clarendon Press, for the extract from *The Allegory of Love*, by C. S. Lewis.

C. G. W.

Let the world pass,
It is ever in dread, and brickle as glass.
The Second Shepherds' Pageant

A man that looks on glass,
On it may stay his eye;
Or if he pleaseth, through it pass,
And then the heaven espy.
George Herbert, *The Elixir*

For now we see through a glass, darkly; but then
face to face: now I know in part; but then shall I
know even as I also am known. And now abideth
faith, hope, charity, these three; but the greatest of
these is charity.
St. Paul, *The First Epistle to the Corinthians*

Guide to Illustrations

PLATES

1. THE TRIUMPHAL ENTRY INTO JERUSALEM

Benedictus qui venit in nomine domini.
Section III, line 220

2. THE TERRORS OF THE PLAGUE AND THE GREAT STORM
Section II, lines 13–15

Transcript: 'XLIX pestilentia. MCterXpenta miseranda ferox violenta. MCCCL . . . superest plebs pessima testis. In fine ij^e [=secundae] ventus validus [? pestis]. . . . [h]oc anno Maurus in orbe tonat MCCCLXI.'

Translation: '[13]49, the plague. 1350, pitiless, fierce, violent. 1350, there survive the dregs of the people to witness. At the end of the second [? outbreak], a mighty wind. In this year, Maur thunders in the world—1361.' St. Maur's day is 15th January.

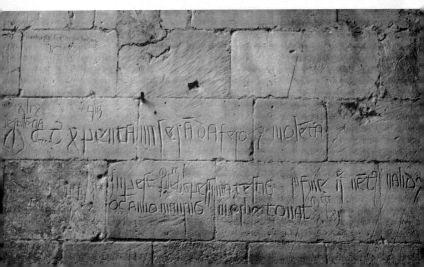

THE CITY OF GOD AND THE CITY OF THE WORLD

I seigh a toure on a toft . . .
Section I, lines 14–18

In the City of God (omitted from this reproduction) appear the Holy Trinity and the Virgin enthroned. Saints are led to the enclosure by the Virtues—Humility, Charity, Patience, Diligence, Mercy, Temperance and Chastity. In the City of the World are shown the works of the Seven Virtues with the works of their opposite Deadly Sins: Diligence and Sloth, Patience and Anger, Charity and Envy, Humility and Pride, Chastity and Lust, Temperance and Gluttony, Generosity and Avarice. Below can be seen seven devils.

4. THE HARROWING OF HELL

'Dukes of this dym place, · anon undo this gates,
That Cryst may come in · the Kynges Sone of Hevene.'

Section III, lines 520–521

General Introduction

TO JUDGE from the number of extant manuscripts[1] (which can represent only a proportion of those originally made) it is clear that in its day *Piers Plowman* was an extremely popular poem; and its popularity continued for a hundred years. Apart from occasional, and sometimes affectionate, references to the book in the sixteenth and seventeenth centuries, however, it was to all intents and purposes forgotten. No edition of the poem appeared between 1561 (Owen Rogers) and 1813 (Whitaker).

Since then, the poem has been increasingly read — though until the present century it has been regarded more often as an ill-catalogued museum of historical snippets than as a poem. But the tide of critical opinion has gathered head over the past forty years, and one no longer has to apologise for the poem.

In the present edition, I have included what I consider to be some of the finest parts of the poem, and I have chosen these with an eye to presenting the reader with sections of sufficiently varied texture to exemplify the versatility of the poet's genius. I have assumed that the reader knows little about the literature of the Middle Ages, and have tried to remedy this deficiency by quotation in the Critical Notes — and as far as possible I have made cross-references to the works of the other great fourteenth-century poet, Geoffrey Chaucer, because good editions of his poems are easily obtainable, and, with Langland, he is one of the most rewarding English authors of the Middle Ages. At times the notes may appear too copious; this has been forced upon me by the difficulty of obtaining the works from which I have drawn information, and thus chapter and page references alone would be of little help to the reader.

I have been constantly aware of the limitations and distortions of meaning of an edition of selections. I agree entirely with Mr. Goodridge[2] that (monotonous as they sometimes are) Langland's long theological discussions were to him matters of intense concern. But it is not easy to appreciate the sharp distinction between

---

[1] There exist more than fifty made before 1500.
[2] J. F. Goodridge, *Piers the Ploughman*, Introduction, p. 53.

subject-matter and style that Mr. Goodridge makes. Few who have experienced the greatness of Langland would doubt that he 'has so much to say of importance, that he would be well worth reading for the matter alone, even if the flavour of his language were entirely lost'; but surely no one would doubt that when Langland feels the 'matter' *most* intensely, or surges forward on the triumphant flood of resolving a long-standing problem, it is expressed in magnificent poetry — and the matter of great poetry is more weighty than that of a prose translation.

It is, then, with Langland at his greatest — that is, with Langland as poet — that this edition is concerned. The entire work appears forbidding in length: I hope that by presenting a little I shall tempt the reader to explore further. An edition of selections has the added disadvantage that the questions which have most interested critics, namely those relating to the structure and pattern of the entire work, are out of our reach. But a whole world of medieval literary thought is not excluded: the forms of church service, the miracle plays, the popular religious works such as the *Golden Legend*, the preaching of homilists. To all these we are introduced as we read the work. It is possible, too, that an abbreviated edition such as this will focus our minds on more detailed study than his lines usually receive. A knowledge of sources, analogues, influences, may help us to see the poem as Langland and his audience saw it; but far more important is appreciation of the wedding of words and thought.

The poetry of *The Vision of William Concerning Piers the Plowman* (to give the work its full name) is for long passages as fine as anything to be found in English literature. Its cumulative effect is powerful and haunting. Great art reaches over the centuries; the intense message of Langland is as relevant to us as to his contemporaries. His appreciation of suffering, of sin, of comedy, of purity, his sensitivity to language and the dramatic management of his scenes fill us with admiration and humility. It is unlikely that a sensitive reader will be unchanged by a reading of the poem.

Langland looks at the complexities of human life, the good, the bad, the great problem of suffering, and he sees an answer. The Dreamer has a vision of Truth and Falsehood and, between them, humanity. Through a lifelong pilgrimage where it is easy to become lost, the Dreamer asks all whom he meets where Truth is. Some give one answer, some another, but little by little the

Dreamer's vision becomes clearer and more intense, and in its final burning focus he sees Jesus on the cross.

His pilgrimage is equally *our* pilgrimage; *we* are part of the crowd in the Field of Folk; for us there is the choice between truth and deceit, between the Spirit of Good and the Spirit of Evil. The Dreamer's questions, for much of the poem, are directed outwards — he observes sin at work in the world. As the poem progresses and his questionings are constantly thwarted, he begins to realize that he must look inwards — and he sees sin at work in himself. It is a matter of beams and motes. The individual conscience — the only member of the Church of Unity to withstand the assaults of Antichrist — is the *sine qua non* in our search for Truth. In a very literal sense, Charity must begin at home.

It is in the qualities I have mentioned that the originality of the poet lies. The notes will make it clear that many of the ideas, and on occasions the very words, are not original in a superficial sense — what ideas are? The commonplaces of sermons, of plays, of political complaints of the people,[1] passages of the Scriptures and of the Liturgy, are all used by Langland as threads to be woven into a great tapestry. I have noted a number of these because it is interesting to see the poet in his workshop as he selects a strand here and a dye there to give form and colour to his creation. Shakespeare did not *invent* the stories of Macbeth and King Lear, but one hardly doubts his originality. He 'found them stone and left them marble'. So, too, with Langland. Sometimes, indeed, Langland relies upon the reader's knowledge of his 'source' to see the pattern of the poem — as in the liturgical pattern of the third section in this edition.

The allegory of the poem may at first prove a stumbling-block to modern readers — unused as we are to allegory. Let us look for a moment at Passus XVIII, where the allegory is made particularly pregnant because two episodes from the New Testament are seen — as, surely, Our Lord intended them to be seen — as one. The story of the Good Samaritan riding on the Jerusalem–Jericho road is indeed the story of Him who rides on the road to Jerusalem on Palm Sunday. Their mission is the same: to suffer for man who has been overcome by the wickedness of the world. After the first reading, where one is probably

[1] Preserved for us in the Rolls of Parliament.

aware only of the *sensus litteralis*, one may re-read and contemplate, and new meanings will emerge *which will not invalidate but
give added depth to the first meaning*.

The road from Jericho to Jerusalem is, on a second plane, the
road of life from an earthly city to a Heavenly one. Mankind,
overcome by sin and helpless, finds that Faith and Hope are
insufficient. Only He who suffers for Mankind and promises a
second coming can help: '. . . the greatest of these is Charity.'
Meanwhile He leaves sinful Mankind at an inn called the New
Testament. The Priest and the Levite were the Old Testament;
but that can help only the prosperous. For the man in adversity,
God Himself must suffer if he is to be saved.

The following table may help the reader to see diagramma-
tically the various elements of the passage:

Jerusalem (the Holy City of Palestine)   = *Heaven*
Jericho (notorious for its evils)   = *Earth*
The Road   = *The Road of Life*
Man (overcome by thieves)   = *Mankind* (overcome by sin)

Abraham	= *Faith*	=	*Levite*	= *Old Testament* (in form)
Spes	= *Hope*	=	*Priest*	= *Old Testament* (in action)
Samaritan ⎫ *Piers* ⎭	= *Charity*	= {	*Samaritan* *Christ*	= *Lex Christi–The New Testament*

All this is simply to rationalize what will become clear as we
read; and dull rationalization cannot make a creative composite
whole of allegory — though many a medieval writer thought it
could! If a medieval preacher says that the five barley loaves
represent the Five Joys of Mary, the symbol is inorganic and
arbitrary. They may just as well have been five wheat loaves —
or five apples. If he says that the man in the ditch represents Mankind, that Piers, the Samaritan, Charity, Christ and the New
Testament are all equally implied at the mention of any one of
them, the connection is natural: the various names stress aspects
of the same thing.

Passus XVIII is complex allegory, where the threads of the
poem are gathered together and form a closely interwoven unity.
Often the allegory is simpler: when Wrath says that he has no
desire to live with monks, the allegorical meaning is simply that
wrath was not a sin which beset the monasteries. One must not
read allegory as if it were a crossword puzzle. Every level of

meaning is the *right* meaning, and if we are reading sympatheti-
cally the other implications will be appreciated simultaneously.
The concision which the allegorical form allows to the description of the Harrowing of Hell makes it one of the most intensely
exciting passages in our literature.

Satire

In literature of satire or complaint, it is impossible to read with
intelligence if we set our texts *in vacuo*. We must know something of the historical and literary background if the full force of
the satire is to come home to us. Madame Eglentyne, in Chaucer's
Prologue to the Canterbury Tales, exemplifies this. If we did not
know that the undertaking of journeys of pilgrimage by nuns was
strictly (and often vainly) forbidden, if we did not know that in
the keeping of dogs, in the mode of wearing of her clothes, in the
possession of her gold brooch, Madame Eglentyne chose to
ignore constant episcopal injunctions, and broke her vows of
poverty and claustration, the whole point of the satire would be
lost. Doubtless, Chaucer intended us to temper justice with
mercy, but for all her coyness and soft lips, his nun is intended
to mirror the decay of ideals in the fourteenth-century nunneries. And if we were uncertain of this, Chaucer ironically
takes a third of his description straight from a passage in the
Roman de la Rose in which the ideal lover's table manners are
detailed.

We have to be on our toes when we read satire — and there is
often a sort of ambivalence which leaves us in doubt as to who is
being mocked. When Belinda in *The Rape of the Lock* smiled, 'all
the world was gay'. Is this simply a flattering hyperbole? Or is 'the
world' the *beau monde*, the only world the pampered Belinda ever
bothers to contemplate? The seemingly innocent, as so often in
satire, may be the flower that shelters the snake.

Satire is an attempt to reform by mockery, and Langland is
one of the great English satirists. Had his Seven Deadly Sins
been as formal and wooden as Marlowe's, Langland's audience
would have been as unmoved as was Faustus. But the Sins in
Piers Plowman are not simply knock-about comedians; they are so
realistic that the readers could see themselves and their society
grotesquely reflected in them. And we, six centuries later, do not
altogether escape censure.

Sermons

Many of the broad outlines Langland doubtless borrowed from the *exempla* of contemporary sermons, in which the medieval mind gave concreteness to abstraction with a facility as great as that with which they frequently saw ultimate and abstract parallels in the concrete. Chaucer's *Pardoner's Tale* is a fine example of medieval preaching in which the theme 'The root of the sins is greed' is given in an illustration, or *exemplum*, so convincing and terrible that even the most worldly in the congregation would go away chastened.

Although Langland is traditional in his descriptions, as in his alliterative verse, the whole is given a vitality that proclaims a creative artist and not a dull imitator or literary parasite. Chaucer's Pardoner describes an inn as a 'develes temple'. This was conventional among contemporary preachers. Langland is more subtle. Gluttony is on his way to church when he is tempted into the inn. We watch the reckless orgy in the ale-house, and we are constantly reminded of the House in which Glutton should be kneeling: 'othes', 'conscience', 'treuthe', 'repented', 'on his knowes', occur in a context of brilliant incongruity. Glutton drinks 'til evensonge', and so much has he drunk that the length of time of his urinating is reckoned as 'a pater-noster while'.

Language

There is much of the colloquial in Langland, as in Bunyan, that is admirably suited to the vigorous characterization, and which reinforces the humour. Phrases which smack of the popularly proverbial come naturally to the characters' lips — Lechery vows 'to drynke but myd the doke', Avarice acknowledges that he is renowned as being 'as hende as hounde is in kychyne'. Again, Avarice is comically (or perhaps pitifully) floored by the word 'restitution', and explains that he thought it meant 'rifling', and he boasts with savage humour that he has 'as moche pite of pore men as pedlere hath of cattes'.

Elsewhere in the poem — in the pathetic prayers for the sick and the poor, and in the description of Christ's Harrowing of Hell — Langland reaches heights of spiritual intensity and poetic magnificence that are sublime.

The poetic form

Chaucer, described by Dryden as 'the father of English poetry', was far less a typically English writer than Langland. Chaucer was European; Langland was English. The verse-form of *Piers Plowman* was essentially the verse-form of the earliest English poetry. The authors of *Beowulf* and *The Battle of Maldon*, or Caedmon himself, traditionally the first English poet, would have recognized in *Piers Plowman* a natural development of their own poetic forms.

> Hige sceal the heardra, · heorte the cenre,
> mod sceal the mare, · the ure mægen lytlath.

The pattern of alliteration (or sometimes of assonance) in Old English verse as — can be seen in the above passage from *The Battle of Maldon* — was very similar to that of *Piers Plowman*. There is in both the basic unit of the half-line and two-accent phrase; the same heightening and tensing of the rhythm in the first half of each line, and the subsequent release, falling in many cases on to the key words in a line:

> He was bitelbrowed · and baberlipped also,
> With two blered eyghen · as a blynde hagge;
> And as a letheren purs · lolled his chekes,
> Wel sydder than his chyn · thei chiveled for elde;
> And as a bondman of his bacoun · his berde was bidraveled.

Langland's verbs and verb formations ('baberlipped', 'lolled', 'chiveled', 'bidraveled') are always full of vitality.

The rhythm of a line is often excellently managed for a special effect:

> there was laughyng and louryng · and 'let go the cuppe'

where the swaying motion imitates the singing of the drunkards in the ale-house. Or the sounds may convey the tones of the speaker's voice, as when Wrath says: 'For she had childe in chirityme · al owre chapitere it wiste.' In this line the vicious whispers of the potager are exactly conveyed in the *sh–ch–ch–ch– iste* of the primary and secondary stresses, as they almost hiss the scandal. For whatever reasons the potager recalls the month, the beauty of 'a childe in chirityme' throws into even stronger relief the vileness of his scandalmongering; though the ill-repute of cherry-fairs lends the words an overtone of sordid innuendo almost as scurrilous as the C-Text reading 'in the chapon-cote' — in the hen-house.

The poet's satiric method

A great deal of the effectiveness of Langland's satire lies in his depiction of sin as physically repellent, and in this he is second only to Swift, 'the great master of disgust'.[1] Sickness and excretions, slimy eyes, lolling cheeks, greasy beards, creeping lice, are all typical of Langland's attempt to show 'scorn her own image, and the very age and body of the time his form and pressure'. And the service in the 'develes temple' contrasts the more strongly with true service, just as the Yahoos contrast with the Houyhnhnms:

> Tyl the daye dawed · this damaiseles daunced,
> That men rongen to the resurexioun · and right with that I waked,
> And called Kitte my wyf · and Kalote my doughter —
> 'Ariseth and reverenceth · Goddes resurrexioun,
> And crepeth to the crosse on knees · and kisseth it for a juwel!
> For Goddes blissed body · it bar for owre bote,
> And it afereth the fende · for suche is the myghte,
> May no grysly gost · glyde there it shadweth!'

But here the similarity between Swift and Langland ends. Both writers have deep sincerity of purpose, but there is more tenderness in Langland. Swift is outraged; Langland bitterly disappointed. Man is often wicked, but 'Goddes mercye is more · than all hise other werkes'.

Langland, like Chaucer, was a reformer not a revolutionary. The similarity of their satiric pictures in the episode of the Seven Deadly Sins and the *General Prologue* is striking. We do not know whether they knew of each other; but it seems more likely that Chaucer knew about the immensely popular *Piers Plowman*, than that Langland had read Chaucer's poetry, written as it was for a considerably smaller and more sophisticated audience. There is some evidence that Piers becomes a symbol of the honest workman and that his tripartite character, assuming into it Jesus Himself *humana natura*, lived in the minds of those who had read, or heard about, the poem. It certainly seems more than coincidental that Chaucer's ideal labourer who works 'for Christes sake', and who loves his neighbours, is a ploughman. And, just as Piers is transformed in the Vita de Dobet into the

[1] So described by Mr. T. S. Eliot in an essay on Andrew Marvell.

ideal priest, so the closeness of this spiritual relationship is paralleled in Chaucer by the physical brotherhood of the Ploughman and the idealized Poor Parson.

That two exact contemporaries, totally different from each other in upbringing, in social status and in literary trends, should both have written great poetic satires of the English society of their time, is a piece of immense fortune. From their writings we know that each man was highly sensitive to all the greatness and weakness of humanity, and, though their satiric methods are different, it is hardly surprising that their judgements are so alike. Once over the initial hurdles of language and notes, we can feel the intensity and fascination of the native allegorical writing; and it is with a shock that we turn to Chaucer and find that his Monk, with his fat swans and gastronomic oaths, is not called Glutton, or that the red-stockinged Wife of Bath has a local habitation, and a name other than Lechery. The age-old alliterative poetry, which for several hundred years had produced little to equal Old English poetry, blossoms splendidly again in the fourteenth century in *Sir Gawain and the Green Knight* and in *Piers Plowman*. But after this, its genius is rebuked by that of the 'modern' poets bringing in the treasures of Renaissance Europe.

The Texts

In 1888 W. W. Skeat demonstrated for the first time that the many manuscripts of *Piers Plowman* were of three main types, which he called the A-, B- and C-Texts. The A-Text (2,500 lines) appears to have been written about 1362. The B-Text is a revision and important expansion of the A-Text, and was probably written about 1377. Poetically, this text is the most impressive. It contains 7,300 lines. The C-Text has a number of alterations of words and arrangement of passages, and may have been written about 1395. It is possible that the C-Text was the revision of someone other than Langland.

The text of the present edition is that of Skeat's *Langland's Vision of Piers Plowman, Text B*, published by the Oxford University Press for the Early English Text Society. The medieval symbols þ and ʒ have, however, in the present edition been replaced by their modern equivalents; and indiscriminate use of *i* and *j*, and of *u* and *v*, has also been normalized. I have not

B

normalized the use of *i* for *y* (and vice versa) because indiscriminate use of these letters does not present a serious visual problem to a modern reader.

The author

It is a strange paradox that of a poem which was in its day so popular there is no certain evidence of authorship.[1] There are two sources of information which I summarize below. (It should be borne in mind that many of the best-known literary works in Old and Middle English were anonymous — no one knows, for example, who wrote *Beowulf* or *Sir Gawain and the Green Knight.*)

Source 1 — Internal. From the poem itself we learn that as a moneyless young man the author came to London from Malvern, and earned a meagre living by saying prayers for the rich. He lived in Cornhill with his wife, Kitty, and daughter, Calotte.[2] Those who knew him regarded him as a fool who devoted his eccentric life to contemplation instead of ingratiating himself with the rich. He grew old and physically weak. He says in the B-text that he is forty-five, and this places his year of birth 1332. He probably died about 1400.

On a number of occasions, he refers to himself as Will; and in one line remarks:

I have lyved in *londe*, quod I · my name is *longe wille*
(my italics).

If the words are read in reverse order, there may be here an example of, not uncommon, medieval name-play.

Source 2 — External. The Trinity College, Dublin, MS in marginal note says that the author, William de Langlond, was a son of Stacy de Rokayle, a gentleman tenant of the Despensers. Stacy lived in Shipton-under-Wychwood, Oxfordshire.

The Huntingdon MS notes: 'Robert or William longland made pers ploughman.'

---

[1] There has been a great deal of discussion on the subject of authorship, much of which arose from the article suggesting composite authorship, written by J. M. Manly in *The Cambridge History of English Literature*. Replies were published in *Modern Philology* by J. J. Jusserand and R. W. Chambers. All the articles have been gathered together in one volume called *The Piers Plowman Controversy*.
[2] See the last six lines of Section III of this edition.

Robert Crowley, the first printer of the poem (1550), says that he had learned that the author was 'Roberte langelande, a Shropshire man borne in Cleybirie about viii myles [it is in fact considerably more] from Maluerne hilles'.[1]

It has been suggested that the poet was a bastard son of Stacy, and took his name from that of a field near the poor home of his mother, and that Stacy provided for him to be educated at Malvern Priory.[2] Later, it is supposed, he took Minor Orders.

SUMMARY OF THE POEM

Part 1: Piers Plowman

The poet, wandering in the Malvern Hills in early summer, lies to rest by a stream and falls asleep. He sees a vision of 'a fair field full of folk', i.e. the world and its inhabitants. The field lies between the Tower of Truth and the Dungeon of Care (Heaven and Hell). A lady, Holy Church, tells the poet that the way to Heaven is through love.

The dreamer sees Falsehood and Flattery with a richly dressed woman, Lady Meed (Reward). She is to be married to Falsehood, but the legality of the wedding is questioned, and the case is taken to the King's court. The King suggests that Lady Meed marry Conscience; but Conscience refuses, and exposes the wickedness of Lady Meed. The trial continues, and Wrong, Wisdom, Peace and others bring various evidence. It has become clear that there are two kinds of meed — God's reward for good works, and corruptly obtained money. The King goes to church and the poet wakes, but soon sleeps again and sees Reason preaching to the people. Repentance helps many of the people (in the form of the Seven Deadly Sins) to ask pardon for their misdeeds, and they make confession.

The penitents set out to seek Truth, but do not know the way until Piers the ploughman offers to guide them, provided that they help him to plough his half-acre. Some shirk their labours and are punished. Truth (God) sends Piers a pardon, and there is much dispute as to its validity.

[1] Crowley's introduction is reproduced in Skeat's E.E.T.S. edition, Preface 2 (Text B), p. xxxii. The place is now called Cleobury Mortimer.

[2] See N. Coghill, *Visions from Piers Plowman*, pp. 127–9.

Part 2 : The Life of Do-wel

After discussion with friars about free-will, the poet sleeps again, and he asks Thought where he may find Do-wel, Do-bet and Do-best. He is introduced to a number of persons, and there follow many theological arguments. Sleeping again, the dreamer sees Lust-of-the-flesh, Lust-of-the-eyes, Fortune, Loyalty and Scripture, and finally a vision of Nature wherein all creatures except man follow Reason.

He meets Imaginative, Conscience, Patience, and Clergy, who is gluttonous. Conscience and Patience leave Clergy and continue on their way. They encounter Haukyn the Active Man, who is a minstrel and wafer-seller. Haukyn's coat is stained with the Seven Deadly Sins. In reply to Conscience's queries, Haukyn explains that he has only one coat. He laments his misdeeds, and the dreamer awakes.

Part 3 : The Life of Do-bet

He dreams again and asks Soul or Reason about the nature of Charity. Soul gives examples, and says that the friars are at this time uncharitable. The poet, fitfully waking and sleeping, still seeks Piers, and meets Abraham (Faith) who also seeks Piers. He then meets Spes (Hope) and they journey towards Jerusalem (allegorically, Heaven). A Samaritan rides near them, and they find a wounded man lying by the roadside 'as naked as a nedle'. Faith and Hope pass by, but the Samaritan (Charity) has pity and leaves the man (Humanity overcome by sin) at an inn called Lex Christi (The New Testament).

Charity, Christ and Piers are seen now as one. In magnificent poetry, Langland describes the Crucifixion, and Christ's descent into Hell and victory over Satan, and the dreamer awakes to hear the Easter bells.

Part 4 : The Life of Do-best

Christ has left the earth and Antichrist appears. In this section, Piers is seen as the church administrator. Pride and Antichrist attack the Church of Unity. Diseases and Death attack mankind. Weary, and hard beset by many enemies, Conscience succeeds in breaking away and he vows a world-wide pilgrimage to seek for Piers the ploughman. The dreamer awakes.

SECTION I

The Field of Folk

Prologue and Passus I

SECTION I

The Field of Folk

To adore, or scorne an image, or protest,
May all be bad; doubt wisely; in strange way
To stand inquiring right, is not to stray;
To sleepe, or runne wrong, is. On a huge hill,
Cragged, and steep, Truth stands, and hee that will
Reach her, about must, and about must goe;
And what the hills suddennes resists, winne so;
Yet strive so, that before age, deaths twilight,
Thy Soule rest, for none can worke in that night.
To wille, implyes delay, therefore now doe.

John Donne, *Satyre III*

In a somer seson · whan soft was the sonne,
I shope me in shroudes · as I a shepe were,
In habite as an heremite · unholy of workes.
Went wyde in this world · wondres to here.
Ac on a May mornynge · on Malverne hulles   5
Me byfel a ferly — · of fairy me thoughte;
I was wery forwandred · and went me to reste
Under a brode banke · bi a bornes side,
And as I lay and lened · and loked in the wateres,
I slombred in a slepyng · it sweyved so merye.   10
    Thanne gan I to meten · a merveilouse swevene,
That I was in a wildernesse — · wist I never where —
As I bihelde in-to the est · an hiegh to the sonne,
I seigh a toure on a toft · trielich ymaked;
A depe dale binethe · a dongeon there-inne,   15
With depe dyches and derke · and dredful of sight;
A faire felde ful of folke · fonde I there bytwene
Of alle maner of men, · the mene and the riche,
Worchyng and wandryng · as the worlde asketh.
Some putten hem to the plow · pleyed ful selde,   20
In settyng and in sowyng · swonken ful harde,

3

And wonnen that wastours · with glotonye destruyeth.
   And some putten hem to pruyde · apparailed hem
     there-after,
In contenaunce of clothyng · comen disgised.
   In prayers and in penance · putten hem manye,   25
Al for love of Owre Lorde · lyveden ful streyte,
In hope forto have · heveneriche blisse;
As ancres and heremites · that holden hem in here selles,
And coveiten nought in contre · to kairen aboute,
For no likerous liflode · her lykam to plese.   30
   And somme chosen chaffare · they cheven the bettere,
As it semeth to owre syght · that suche men thryveth;
And somme murthes to make · as mynstralles conneth,
And geten gold with here glee · synneles, I leve.
Ac japers and jangelers, · Judas chylderen,   35
Feynen hem fantasies · and foles hem maketh,
And han here witte at wille · to worche yif thei sholde.
That Poule precheth of hem · I nel nought preve it here;
Qui turpiloquium loquitur · is Luciferes hyne.
   Bidders and beggeres · fast aboute yede,   40
With her bely and her bagges · of bredful ycrammed;
Fayteden for here fode, · foughten atte ale;
In glotonye, God it wote · gon hii to bedde,
And risen with ribaudye · tho roberdes knaves;

39: He who speaks lewdly.

Slepe and sori-sleuthe · seweth hem evre.   45
   Pilgrymes and palmers · plighted hem togidere
To seke seynt James · and seyntes in Rome.
Thei went forth in here wey · with many wise tales,
And hadden leve to lye · al here lyf after.
I seigh somme that seiden · thei had ysought seyntes;   50
To eche a tale that thei tolde · here tonge was tempred to lye,
More than to sey soth · it semed bi here speche.
   Heremites on an heep · with hoked staves,
Wenten to Walsyngham · and here wenches after;
Grete lobyes and longe · that loth were to swynke,   55
Clotheden hem in copis · to ben knowen fram othere;
And shopen hem heremites · here ese to have.
   I fonde there Freris · alle the foure ordres,
Preched the peple · for profit of hem-selven,
Glosed the gospel · as hem good lyked.   60
For coveitise of copis · construed it as thei wolde.
Many of this maistres Freris · mowe clothen hem at lykyng,
For here money and marchandise · marchen togideres.
For sith charite hath be chapman · and chief to shryve lordes,
Many ferlis han fallen · in a fewe yeris.   65
But holychirche and hii · holde better togideres,
The moste myschief on molde · is mountyng wel faste.
   There preched a Pardonere · as he a prest were,
Broughte forth a bulle · with bishopes seles,
And seide that hym-self myghte · assoilen hem alle   70
Of falshed of fastyng · of vowes ybroken.
   Lewed men leved hym wel · and lyked his wordes,
Comen up knelyng · to kissen his bulles;
He bonched hem with his brevet · and blered here eyes,
And raughte with his ragman · rynges and broches.   75
Thus they geven here golde · glotones to kepe,
And leveth such loseles · that lecherye haunten.
Were the bischop yblissed · and worth bothe his eres,
His seel shulde nought be sent · to deceyve the peple.
Ac it is naught by the bischop · that the boy precheth,   80
For the parisch prest and the pardonere · parten the silver,

That the poraille of the parisch · sholde have yif thei nere.
   Persones and parisch prestes · pleyned hem to the bischop,
That here parisshes were pore · sith the pestilence tyme,
To have a lycence and a leve · at London to dwelle,   85
And syngen there for symonye, · for silver is swete.
   Bischopes and bachelers, · bothe maistres and doctours,
That han cure under Criste · and crounyng in tokne
And signe that thei sholden · shryven here paroschienes,
Prechen and prey for hem · and the pore fede,   90
Liggen in London · in lenten, an elles.
Somme serven the kyng · and his silver tellen,
In cheker and in chancerye · chalengen his dettes
Of wardes and wardmotes, · weyves and streyves.
   And some serven as servants · lordes and ladyes,   95
And in stede of stuwardes · sytten and demen.
Here messe and here matynes · and many of here oures
Arn don undevoutlych; · drede is at the laste
Lest Crist in consistorie · acorse ful manye.
I parceyved of the power · that Peter had to kepe,   100
To bynde and to unbynde · as the boke telleth,
How he it left with love · as Owre Lorde hight,
Amonges foure vertues · the best of alle vertues,
That cardinales ben called · and closyng gatis,
There Crist is in kyngdome · to close and to shutte,   105
And to opne it to hem · and hevene blisse shewe.
Ac of the cardinales atte Courte · that caught of that name,
And power presumed in hem · a Pope to make,
To han that power that Peter hadde · inpugnen I nelle;
For in love and letterure · the eleccioun bilongeth,   110
For-thi I can and can naughte · of courte speke more.
Thanne come there a kyng, · knyghthod hym ladde,
Might of the comunes · made hym to regne,
And thanne cam Kynde Wytte · and clerkes he made,
For to conseille the kyng · and the comune save.   115
   The kyng and knyghthode · and clergye bothe
Casten that the comune · shulde hem-self fynde.
   The comune contreved · of Kynde Witte craftes,

And for profit of alle the poeple · plowmen ordeygned,
To tilie and travaile · as trewe lyf asketh.   120
The kynge and the comune · and Kynde Witte the thridde
Shope lawe and lewte · eche man to knowe his owne.

    Thanne loked up a lunatik, · a lene thing with-alle,
And knelyng to the kyng · clergealy he seyde:
'Crist kepe the, sire kyng, · and thi kyngriche,   125
And leve the lede thi londe · so leute the lovye
And for thi rightful rewlyng · be rewarded in hevene!'

      *   *   *   *   *

    Yit hoved there an hondreth · in houves of selke,
Serjaunts it semed · that serveden atte barre,
Plededen for penyes · and poundes the lawe,   130
And nought for love of Owre Lorde · unlese here lippes
    onis.
Thow myghtest better mete the myste · on Malverne hulles,
Than gete a momme of here mouthe · but money were
    shewed.
    Barones an burgeis · and bonde-men als
I seigh in this assemble · as ye shul here after.   135
Baxsteres and brewesteres · and bocheres manye,
Wollewebsteres · and weveres of lynnen,
Taillours and tynkeres · and tolleres in marketes,
Masons and mynours · and many other craftes.
Of alkin libbyng laboreres · lopen forth somme,   140
As dykers and delveres · that doth here dedes ille,
And dryven forth the longe day · with 'Dieu vous save, Dame
    Emme!'
Cokes and here knaves · crieden, 'hote pies, hote!
Gode gris and gees · gowe dyne, gowe!'
    Taverners un-til hem · tolde the same,   145
'White wyn of Oseye · and red wyn of Gascoigne,
Of the Ryne and of the Rochel · the roste to defye.' —
Al this seigh I slepyng · and sevene sythes more.

142: 'God preserve you, mistress Emma!'

WHAT THIS montaigne bymeneth · and the merke
    dale,
And the felde ful of folke · I shal yow faire schewe.   150
A loveli ladi of lere · in lynnen yclothed,
Come down fram a castel · and called me faire,
And seide, 'Sone, slepestow?' · Sestow this poeple,
How bisi thei ben · abouten the mase?
The moste partie of this poeple · that passeth on this
    erthe,   155
Have thei worschip in this worlde, · thei wilne no better;
Of other hevene than here · holde thei no tale.'
    I was aferd of her face · theigh she faire were,
And seide, 'Mercy, Madame · what is this to mene?'
'The toure up the toft,' quod she, · 'Treuthe is there-
    inne,   160
And wolde that ye wroughte · as his worde techeth;
For he is fader of feith · fourmed yow alle,
Bothe with fel and with face · and yaf yow fyve wittis
Forto worschip hym ther-with · the while that ye ben
    here.
And therfore he hyghte the erthe · to help yow uchone   165
Of wollen, of lynnen, · of lyflode at nede,
In mesurable manere · to make yow at ese;
    And comaunded of his curteisye · in comune three
        thinges;
Arne none nedful but tho, · and nempne hem I thinke,
And rekne hem bi resoun · reherce thow hem after.   170
That one is vesture · from chele the to save,
And mete atte mele · for myseise of thi-selve,
And drynke whan thow dryest — · ac do nought out of
    resoun:
That thow worth the werse · whan thow worche shuldest.
    For Loth in his lifdayes · for likyng of drynke,   175
Dede bi his doughtres · that the devel lyked;
Delited hym in drynke · as the devel wolde,
And lecherye hym laught, · and lay bi hem bothe;
And al he witt it wyn · that wikked dede.

Inebriamus eum vino, dormiamusque cum eo,
ut servare possimus de patre nostro semen.

Thorw wyn and thorw women · there was Loth acombred,
And there gat in glotonye · gerlis that were cherlis.   181
For-thi drede delitable drynke · and thow shalt do the
    bettere;
Mesure is medcyne · though thow moche yerne.
It is naught al gode to the goste · that the gutte axeth,
Ne liflode to thi likam · that leef is to thi soule.   185
Leve not thi likam · for a lyer him techeth,
That is the wrecched worlde · wolde the bitraye.
For the fende and thi flesch · folweth the to-gidere,
This and that sueth thi soule · and seith it in thin herte;
And for thow sholdest ben ywar · I wisse the the beste.'   190
    'Madame, mercy,' quod I, · 'me liketh wel yowre
    wordes,
Ac the moneye of this molde · that men so faste holdeth,
Telle me to whom, Madame, · that tresore appendeth?'
    'Go to the gospel,' quod she, · 'that God seide hym-
    selven,
Tho the poeple hym apposed · with a peny in the temple,   195
Whether thei shulde ther-with · worschip the kyng Sesar.
And God axed of hem · of whome spake the lettre,
And the ymage ilyke · that there-inne stondeth.
"Cesaris," thei seide, · "we sen hym wel uchone."
    "*Reddite cesari*", quod God · "that *cesari* bifalleth,   200
Et que sunt dei, deo · or elles ye done ille."
For rightful reson · shulde rewle yow alle,
And kynde witte be wardeyne · yowre welthe to kepe,
And tutour of youre tresore · and take it yow at nede;
For housbonderye and hii · holden togideres.'   205
Thanne I frained hir faire, · for Hym that hir made,
'That dongeoun in the dale · that dredful is of sighte,

179: Let us make him drunk with wine, and let us sleep with him,
that we may be able to preserve the seed of our father.

200–1: 'Render unto Caesar', said God, 'those things that belong to
Caesar, and those things that are God's, to God.'

What may it be to mene, · ma-dame, I yow biseche?'
'That is the Castel of Care; who-so cometh therinne
May banne that he borne was · to body or to soule.   210
Therinne wonieth a wighte · that Wronge is yhote,
Fader of Falshed · and founded it hym-selve.
Adam and Eve · he egged to ille,
Conseilled Caym · to kullen his brother;
Judas he japed · with Juwen silver,   215
And sithen on an eller · honged hym after.
He is letter of love · and lyeth hem alle,
That trusten on his tresor · bitrayeth he sonnest.'
    Thanne had I wonder in my witt · what womman it were
That such wise wordes · of holy writ shewed;   220
And asked hir on the hieghe name, · ar heo thennes yeode,
What she were witterli · that wissed me so faire.
    'Holicherche I am,' quod she, · 'thow oughtest me to
            knowe,
I underfonge the firste · and the feyth taughte,
And broughtest me borwes · my biddyng to fulfille,   225
And to love me lelly · the while thi lyf dureth.'
    Thanne I courbed on my knees · and cryed hir of grace,
And preyed hir pitousely · prey for my synnes,
And also kenne me kyndeli · on Criste to bileve,
That I might worchen his wille · that wroughte me to man;
'Teche me to no tresore, · but telle me this ilke,   231
How I may save my soule, · that seynt art yholden?'
    'Whan alle tresores aren tried,' quod she, · 'trewthe is the
            best;
I do it on *deus caritas* · to deme the sothe;
It is as derworth a drewery · as dere God hym-selven.   235
Who-so is trewe of his tonge · and telleth none other,
And doth the werkis ther-with · and wilneth no man ille,
He is a god bi the gospel, · agrounde and aloft,
And ylike to Owre Lorde, · bi seynte Lukes wordes.
The clerkes that knoweth this · shulde kenne it aboute,   240
For cristene and uncristne · clameth it uchone.
            234: I appeal to the text 'God is love'.

Kynges and knightes · shulde kepe it bi resoun,
Riden and rappe down, · in reumes aboute,
And taken *trangressores* · and tyen hem faste,
Til treuthe had ytermyned · her trespas to the ende.   245
And that is the professioun appertly · that appendeth for
    knyghtes,
And nought to fasten a fryday · in fyve score wynter;
But holden with him and with hir · that wolden al treuthe,
And never leve hem for love · ne for lacchyng of sylver.'

244: transgressors.

SECTION II

The Seven Deadly Sins

Passus V–VI

SECTION II

The Seven Deadly Sins

Wilt thou forgive that sin, by which I'have won
Others to sin, and made my sin their door?
Wilt thou forgive that sin which I did shun
A year or two, but wallowed in a score?
When thou hast done, thou hast not done,
 For I have more.

John Donne, *Hymn to God the Father*

THE CONCEPT of man's wandering in a world where there were seven particular spirits of evil eager to defile him was a commonplace in England in the later Middle Ages. Often these spirits were thought of as demons in animal form, and any sins which were not specifically mentioned among the Seven were shown to be their bestial offspring.[1]

It is probable that the idea owes its origin to the fusion of Eastern and Western beliefs which followed the conquests of Alexander.[2] In the early centuries A.D., a number of heretical Hellenistic sects, particularly the Gnostics, paid great attention to Oriental accounts of the Soul Drama — that is, the journey of the soul, either pre-natal, during life (in mystical trance) or after death, to or from the Eighth Sphere of spiritual perfection. There were beliefs that the remaining seven spheres were each dominated by a particular demon who contaminated the souls that passed by them on their way to Earth. As the concept developed, a distinct sin was attributed to each demon, and the conventional list of Seven Cardinal Sins was slowly standardized, as, too, was the order in which they were listed.

In Ireland in the seventh and eighth centuries, the list of Seven Cardinal Sins was, because of its convenience as an easily

[1] See note on l. 160 of Section III of this edition, especially passage quoted from the *Ancrene Wisse*.
[2] I am indebted for much of the information here given to *The Seven Deadly Sins* by Professor Morton W. Bloomfield. Of particular interest is the chapter 'The Cardinal Sins in *The Divine Comedy* and in English Literature of the Fourteenth Century'.

remembered and comprehensive catalogue, employed by confessional priests. Through their increased, and later very common, association with the Confessional, arose the idea of Seven Deadly Sins.[1]

Particularly in the fourteenth century, the concept was widely popularized not only by the Confessional, but also in drama[2] and in sermons,[3] in carvings and in paintings.[4] Chaucer's *Parson's Tale* is a prose sermon on the popular twin themes of penance and the Seven Sins.

What matters to us is how Langland treats the conventions. He uses most of them — the penitential setting, the comments on contemporary evil practices, the usual order in which the sins appear, even some of the animals by which they were commonly symbolized — the adder in Envy and the pig in Gluttony. But Langland's presentation of the sins has no rivals in our tongue. So much that in others had been accretion and paraphernalia in the tradition, becomes in Langland incisive, vital to his creation. Look, for example, at the tedious animal list in the *Ancrene Wisse*: 'The lion of Pride slays all the proud, all that are conceited and proud in heart; the venomous adder slays etc.' There is nothing organic in these words; they are meaningless formulae.[5] Contrast with this the ill effects of over-indulgence in drink on Glutton: 'His guts gurgled away like a couple of greedy sows.' The germ of the animal tradition is there, and in Langland it has sprung to new life.

In some of the homilists there is writing on the subject that is

[1] A *cardinal* sin is a chief or important sin; a *deadly* sin is one that would bring final damnation if unconfessed and unrepented. In the later Middle Ages the distinction was not always made clear. In the thirteenth century, St. Thomas Aquinas refers to the Seven as cardinal. Cf. line 20 of this Section.

[2] See, for example, note on Section I, line 3 in this edition.

[3] G. R. Owst in *Literature and Pulpit in Medieval England* gives many quotations from the passages dealing with the Seven Deadly Sins in medieval homilies. Some of these I have mentioned in the notes on this section, but the long passages in *Literature and Pulpit* should be consulted if the reader wishes to see how Langland would have heard of the sins from the preachers of his day.

[4] See M. D. Anderson, *Drama and Imagery in English Medieval Churches*.

[5] In fairness, it must be remembered that the *Ancrene Wisse* was written some 150 years before *Piers Plowman*; and the scenes with the Seven Deadly Sins that follow the animal list in that text are remarkably lively.

terse and vigorous; but, as so often in sermonizing then as now, it is frequently marred by a deep seriousness that is pedagogic and insists on being exhaustive. The unfailing high seriousness of Langland allows him to laugh, to scoff, to pity, without the fear that his moral purpose is being obscured.

He is no automatic writer, huddling together the recognized constituent parts and producing imitation poetry: we have in this passage absolute confidence in the creator. If Wrath appears as a friar at one moment, as a potager in a convent at another, as an outcast monk a line or two further on, we are held by the dramatic illusion and the moral implication is clear. Glutton is an obvious masterpiece — perhaps the very crudeness of its comedy implies a mind behind it all that is devoid of the primness of many a homilist — the coarse, gross Glutton at whose excesses there is nothing but laughter and mockery is so much the more a grim warning against a sin that degrades man to the level of a gleeman's bitch. Excellent, too, in its brevity is the reaction of Sloth: ' "Haven't you repented at all?" asked Repentance, and Sloth fell asleep instantly.' In this example, there is double-edged implication: is it simple comedy, or an allegorical description of the immediate reaction on the part of idle priests when the suggestion of repentance occurred to them? It is, both in verbal pattern and in implication, of a kind with that superbly scornful line (not in the present edition) where the Dreamer questions a Doctor of Theology. Patience and the Dreamer are eating humbly at a low table, while the Doctor is feasting at the high table. Asked whether he can tell the two anything about the life of Do-Well, he replies — ' "Do-well?" said this Doctor — and took the cup and drank.'

In the passage where the Sins confess, we see a living and satirical picture of fourteenth-century England, and it is more pertinent to think of it in the way we think of *The Prologue to the Canterbury Tales* than as an offspring of a mnemonic list for contemporary priests. This point can be seen more clearly if one reads through the description of the procession of the Sins in *The Faerie Queene*.[1] The moments of good writing there — and Spenser is capable of fine writing — are blurred in two ways. First, the allegorical figures remain as abstractions; when we read the passage we can see Envy, but it requires a conscious

[1] *Faerie Queene*, Book I, Canto iv.

intellectual shift to recognize that he is a vital and present being, such-and-such a politician, or priest, or oneself. And if the intellectual shift has to be as conscious as this, the writing is not allegory at all but imitation allegory. Second, the passage is spoiled by sheer arithmetic — we find ourselves ticking off the riders in the procession, with something of the relief that is felt when any list is nearing its end. Spenser's invention, too, one imagines was wearing thin at that point — 'And by his side rode . . .'; 'And next to him rode . . .'; 'And greedy Avarice by him did ride . . .'; 'And next to him malicious Envy rode . . .'; 'And him beside rode . . .' So also with the conventional animal associations: they are all there, but they are not functional and even require explanation:

> And next to him rode lustfull *Lechery*,
> Vpon a bearded Goat, whose rugged haire,
> And whally eyes (the signe of gelosy,)
> Was like the person selfe, whom he did beare.

In spite of these weaknesses, Spenser's description has, of course, much that is admirable; and I give this amount of attention to his treatment of the subject simply to pinpoint some of the major dangers inherent in a list of this kind, so that we can be more fully aware of the greatness of Langland's achievement. One feels that the material of Spenser's procession is general observation from life and perhaps more detailed observation from literature. Langland gives the impression of a man who has lingered at the fairs at Weyhill and Winchester, in the alleys and ale-houses of London, observing in passionate detail, now with tenderness, now with revulsion, sinful mankind. The urgency of his mission to love Truth with all his heart and mind and soul forced him to demand that his words and characters should live — for he knew that the Sins were no poetical fancies, but that part of man that degrades and debases.

> The kyng and his knightes · to the kirke wente
> To here matynes of the day · and the masse after.
> Thanne waked I of my wynkynge · and wo was with-alle,
> That I ne hadde sleped sadder · and yseyen more.
> Ac er I hadde faren a fourlonge · feyntise me hente, 5
> That I ne myghte ferther a-foot · for defaute of slepynge;

And sat softly adown · and seide my bileve,
And so I babeled on my bedes · thei broughte me a-slepe.
    And thanne saw I moche more · than I bifore tolde,
For I say the felde ful of folke · that I bifore of seyde,   10
And how Resoun gan arrayen hym · alle the reume to preche,
And with a crosse afor the kynge · comsed thus to techen.
    He preved that thise pestilences · were for pure synne,
And the southwest wynde · on Saterday at evene
Was pertliche for pure pryde · and for no poynt elles.   15
Piries and plomtrees · were puffed to the erthe,
In ensample, ye segges, · ye shulden do the bettere.
Beches and brode okes · were blowen to the grounde,
Torned upward her tailles · in tokenynge of drede,
That dedly synne at domesday · shal fordon hem alle.   20
    Of this matere I myghte · mamely ful longe,
Ac I shal seye as I saw, · so me God helpe!
How pertly afor the poeple · Resoun gan to preche.
    He bad Wastoure go worche · what he best couthe,
And wynnen his wastyng · with somme manere crafte.   25
    And preyed Peronelle · her purfyle to lete,
And kepe it in hir cofre · for catel at hire nede.
    Thomme Stowue he taughte · to take two staves,
And fecche Felice home · fro the wyven pyne.
    He warned Watt · his wyf was to blame,   30
That hire hed was worth halve a marke, · his hode noughte
    worth a grote.
And bad Bette kut · a bow other tweyne,
And bete Betoun ther-with · but if she wolde worche.
And thanne he charged chapmen · to chasten her childeren;
Late no wynnynge hem forweny · whil thei be yonge,   35
Ne for no pouste of pestilence · plese hem noughte out of
    resoun.
    'My syre seyde so to me, · and so did my dame,
That the levere childe · the more lore bihoveth,
And Salamon seide the same · that Sapience made,
        Qui parcit virge, odit filium.
            39: He who spares the rod, hates the child.

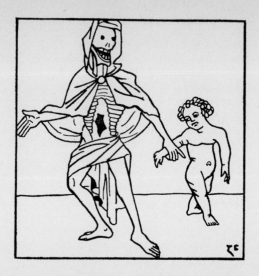

The Englich of this Latyn is, · who-so wil it knowe, 40
Who-so spareth the sprynge · spilleth his children.'
   And sithen he preyed prelats · and prestes to-gideres,
'That ye prechen to the peple · preve it on yowre-selven,
And doth it in dede · it shal drawe yow to good;
If ye lyven as ye leren us · we shal leve yow the bettere.' 45
   And sithen he radde Religioun · here reule to holde—
'Leste the kynge and his conseille · yowre comunes appayre,
And ben stuwardes of yowre stedes · til ye be ruled bettre.'
And sithen he conseilled the kynge · the comune to lovye,
'It is thi tresore, if tresoun ne were · and triacle at thi nede.'
And sithen he prayed the pope · have pite on holicherche, 51
And er he gyve any grace · governe firste hym-selve.
   'And ye that han lawes to kepe · late treuthe be yowre
      coveytise,
More than golde or other gyftes, if ye wil God plese;
For who-so contrarieth treuthe · he telleth in the gospel, 55
That God knoweth hym noughte · ne no seynte of hevene,
    Amen dico vobis, nescio vos.

     56: Verily, I say unto you, I do not know you.

And ye that seke Seynte James · and seintes of Rome,
Seketh Seynt Treuthe, · for he may save yow alle;
Qui cum patre & filio · that feire hem bifalle
That suweth my sermon.' · And thus seyde Resoun. 60
Thanne ran Repentance · and reherced his teme,
And gert Wille to wepe · water with his eyen.

SUPERBIA

Peronelle Proude-herte · platte hir to the erthe,
And lay longe ar she loked · and 'Lorde, mercy!' cryed,
And byhighte to Hym · that us alle made, 65
She shulde unsowen hir serke · and sette there an heyre
To affaiten hire flesshe · that fierce was to synne:
'Shal nevere heighe herte me hente · but holde me lowe,
And suffre to be myssayde — · and so did I nevere.
But now wil I meke me · and mercy biseche, 70
For al this I have · hated in myne herte.'

LUXURIA

Thanne Lecchoure seyde 'allas!' · and on Owre Lady he
    cryed,
To make mercy for his mis-dedes · bitwene God and his
    soule,
With that he shulde the Saterday · sevene yere there-after,
Drynke but myd the doke · and dyne but ones. 75

INVIDIA

Envye with hevy herte · asked after scrifte,
And carefullich *mea culpa* · he comsed to shewe.
He was as pale as a pelet, · in the palsye he semed,
And clothed in a caurimaury, · I couthe it noughte discreve;
In kirtel and kourteby · and a knyf bi his syde, 80

59: Who with the Father and the Son. . . .
77: Mine is the blame.

Of a freres frokke · were the forsleves.
And as a leke hadde yleye · longe in the sonne,
So loked he with lene chekes · lourynge foule.
  His body was to-bolle for wratthe · that he bote his lippes,
And wryngynge he yede with the fiste, · to wreke hymself he
      thoughte,   85
With werkes or with wordes · when he seighe his tyme.
Eche a worde that he warpe · was of an addres tonge,
Of chydynge and of chalangynge · was his chief lyflode,
With bakbitynge and bismer · and beryng of fals witnesse;
This was al his curteisye · where that evere he shewed hym.
  'I wolde ben yshryve,' quod this schrewe, · 'and I for shame
      durst;   91
I wolde be gladder, bi God · that Gybbe had meschaunce,
Than thoughe I had this woke ywonne · a weye of Essex
      chese.
I have a neighbore neyghe me, · I have ennuyed hym ofte,
And lowen on hym to lordes · to don hym lese his silver,   95
And made his frendes ben his foon · thorw my false tonge;
His grace and his good happes · greveth me ful sore.
Bitwene many and many · I make debate ofte,
That bothe lyf and lyme · is lost thorw my speche.
And when I mete him in market · that I moste hate,   100
I hailse hym hendeliche, · as I his frende were;
For he is doughtier than I, · I dar do non other.
Ac hadde I maystrye and myghte, · God wote my wille!
  And whan I come to the kirke · and sholde knele to the
      Rode,
And preye for the pople · as the prest techeth,   105
For pilgrimes and for palmers · for alle the poeple after,
Thanne I crye on my knees · that Cryste yif hem sorwe
That baren awey my bolle · and my broke schete.
  Awey fro the auter thanne · turne I myn eyghen,
And biholde how Eleyne · hath a newe cote;   110
I wisshe thanne it were myne · and al the webbe after.
  And of mennes lesynge I laughe · that liketh myn herte;
And for her wynnynge I wepe · and waille the tyme,

And deme that hii don ille · there I do wel worse;
Who-so undernymeth me here-of · I hate hym dedly
    after.   115
I wolde that uche a wyght · were my knave,
For who-so hath more than I · that angreth me sore.
And thus I lyve lovelees, lyke a luther dogge,
That al my body bolneth · for bitter of my galle.
    I myghte noughte eet many yeres · as a man oughte,   120
For envye and yvel wille · is yvel to defye;
May no sugre ne swete thinge · asswage my swellynge,
Ne no diapenidion · dryve it fro myne herte,
Ne noyther schrifte ne shame, · but ho-so schrape my
    mawe?'
    'Yus, redili,' quod Repentaunce, · and radde hym to the
    beste,   125
'Sorwe of synnes · is savacioun of soules.'
    'I am sori,' quod that segge, · 'I am but selde other,
And that maketh me thus megre · for I ne may me venge.
Amonges burgeyses have I be · dwellynge at Londoun,
And gert bakbitinge be a brocoure · to blame mennes ware.
Whan he solde and I noughte · thanne was I redy   131
To lye and to loure on my neighbore · and to lakke his
    chaffare.
I wil amende this, yif I may, · thorw myghte of God
    Almyghty.'

IRA

    Now awaketh Wratthe · with two whyte eyen,
And nyvelynge with the nose · and his nekke hangynge.   135
    'I am Wrath,' quod he, · 'I was sum tyme a frere,
And the coventes Gardyner · for to graffe ympes;
On limitoures and listres · lesynges I ymped,
Tyl thei bere leves of low speche · lordes to plese,
And sithen thei blosmed obrode · in boure to here
    shriftes.   140
And now is fallen ther-of a frute · that folke han wel levere

Schewen her shcriftes to hem · than shryve hem to her
    persones.
  And now persones han parceyved · that Freres parte with
    hem,
Thise possessioneres preche · and deprave freres,
And freres fyndeth hem in defaute, · as folke bereth
    witnes,   145
That whan thei preche the poeple · in many place aboute,
I, Wrath, walke with hem · and wisse hem of my bokes.
Thus thei speken of spiritualte · that eyther despiseth other,
Til thei be bothe beggers · and by my spiritualte libben,
Or elles alle riche · and riden aboute.   150
I, Wrath, rest nevere · that I ne moste folwe
This wykked folke, · for suche is my grace.
  I have an aunte to nonne · and an abbesse bothe,
Hir were levere swowe or swelte · than suffre any peyne.
I have be cook in hir kichyne · and the covent served   155
Many monthes with hem · and with monkes bothe.
I was the priouresses potagere · and other poure ladyes,
And made hem joutes of jangelynge · that dame Johanne was
    a bastard,
And dame Clarice a knightes doughter, · ac a kokewolde was
    hire syre,
And dame Peronelle a prestes file, · Priouresse worth she
    nevere,   160
For she had childe in chirityme — · al owre chapitere it wiste.
  Of wykked wordes I, Wrath, · here wortes i-made,
Til "thow lixte" and "thow lixte" · lopen oute at ones,
And eyther hitte other · under the cheke;
Hadde thei had knyves, bi Cryst, · her eyther had killed
    other.   165
  Seynt Gregorie was a gode pope · and had a gode forwit,
That no priouresse were prest, · for that he ordeigned.
Thei had thanne ben *infamis* the firste day, · thei can so yvel
    hele conseille.
Amonge monkes I mighte be, · ac many tyme I shonye;

168: Of poor reputation.

For there ben many felle frekis · my feres to aspye,   170
Bothe Prioure an supprioure · and owre *pater abbas*;
And if I telle any tales · thei taken hem togyderes,
And do me faste Frydayes · to bred and to water,
And am chalanged in the chapitelhous · as I a childe were,
And baleised on the bare ers · and no breche bitwene;   175
For-thi have I no lykyng · with tho leodes to wonye.
I ete there unthende fisshe · and fieble ale drynke;
Ac other while, whan wyn cometh, · whan I drynke wyn at
        eve,
I have a fluxe of a foule mouthe · wel fyve dayes after.
Al the wikkednesse that I wote · bi any of owre
        bretheren,   180
I couth it in owre cloistre · that al owre covent wote it.'
        'Now repent the,' quod Repentaunce, · 'and reherce thow
        nevre
Conseille that thow cnowest · bi contenaunce ne bi righte;
And drynke noughte over delicatly, · ne to depe noyther,
That thi wille bi cause ther-of · to wrath myghte torne.   185
Esto sobrius,' he seyde, · and assoilled hym after,
And bad hym wilne to wepe · his wikkednesse to amende.

AVARICIA

        And thanne cam Coveytise, · can I hym noughte descryve,
So hungriliche and holwe · Sire Hervy hym loked.
He was bitelbrowed · and baberlipped also,   190
With two blered eyghen · as a blynde hagge;
And as a letheren purs · lolled his chekes,
Wel sydder than his chyn · thei chiveled for elde;
And as a bondman of his bacoun · his berde was bidraveled.
With an hode on his hed · a lousi hatte above,   195
In a tauny tabarde · of twelve wynter age,
Al totorne and baudy · and ful of lys crepynge;
But if that a lous couthe · have lopen the bettre,

        171: Father Abbot.   186: Be sober.

She sholde noughte have walked on that welche · so was it
    thredebare.
   'I have ben Coveytouse,' quod this caityve, · 'I bi-knowe
    it here;   200
For some tyme I served · Symme atte Stile,
And was his prentis yplighte · his profit to wayte.
First I lerned to lye · a leef other tweyne,
Wikkedlich to weye · was my furst lessoun.
To Wy and to Wynchestre · I went to the faire,   205
With many manere marchandise, · as my maistre me highte;
Ne had the grace of gyle · ygo amonge my ware,
It had be unsolde this sevene yere, · so me God helpe!
   Thanne drowe I me amonges draperes · my donet to lerne,
To drawe the lyser alonge · the lenger it semed;   210
Amonge the riche rayes · I rendred a lessoun,
To broche hem with a pak-nedle · and plaited hem togyderes,
And put hem in a presse · and pynned hem therinne,
Tyl ten yerdes or twelve · hadde tolled out threttene.
   My wyf was a webbe · and wollen cloth made;   215
She spak to spynnesteres · to spynnen it oute.
Ac the pounde that she payed by · poised a quarteroun
    more,
Than myne owne auncere, · who-so weyghed treuthe.
   I boughte hir barly malte, · she brewe it to selle;
Peny ale and podyng ale · she poured togideres   220
For laboreres and for low folke, · that lay by hymselve.
   The best ale lay in my boure · or in my bedchambre,
And who-so bummed ther-of · boughte it ther-after,
A galoun for a grote, · Gode wote, no lesse;
And yit it cam in cupmel, · this crafte my wyf used.   225
Rose the regratere · was hir righte name;
She hath holden hokkerye · al hire lyf tyme.
   Ac I swere now, so the ik, · that synne wil I lete,
And nevere wikkedliche weye · ne wikke chaffare use,
But wenden to Walsyngham · and my wyf als,   230
And bidde the Rode of Bromeholme · brynge me oute of
    dette.'

'Repentedestow the evere,' quod Repentance, · 'ne
    restitucioun madest?'
'Yus, ones I was herberwed,' quod he, · 'with an hep of
    chapmen,
I roos whan thei were arest · and yrifled here males.'
'That was no restitucioun,' quod Repentance, · 'but a
    robberes thefte,   235
Thow haddest be better worthy · be hanged therfore
Than for al that · that thow hast here shewed.'
'I wende ryflynge were restitucioun,' quod he, · 'for I lerned
    nevere rede on boke,
And I can no Frenche in feith, · but of the ferthest ende of
    Norfolke.'
'Usedestow evere usurie,' quod Repentaunce, · 'in alle
    thi lyf tyme?'   240
'Nay, sothly,' he seyde, · 'save in my youthe.
I lerned amonge Lumbardes · and Jewes a lessoun,
To wey pens with a peys · and pare the hevyest,
And lene it for love of the crosse · to legge a wedde and lese it;
Suche dedes I did wryte · yif he his day breke.   245
I have mo maneres thorw rerages · than thorw *miseretur &*
    comodat.
    I have lent lordes · and ladyes my chaffare,
And ben her brocour after · and boughte it my-self.
Eschaunges and chevesances · with suche chaffare I dele,
And lene folke that lese wol · a lyppe at every noble.   250
And with lumbardes lettres · I ladde golde to Rome,
And toke it by taille here · and tolde hem there lasse.'
'Lentestow evere lordes · for love of her mayntenaunce?'
'Ye, I have lent lordes · loved me nevere after,
And have ymade many a knyghte · bothe mercere and
    drapere,   255
That payed nevere for his prentishode · nought a peire
    gloves.'
'Hastow pite on pore men · that mote nedes borwe?'

246: [A good man] pities and lends.

'I have as moche pite of pore men · as pedlere hath of
    cattes,
That wolde kille hem, yf he cacche hem myghte, · for
    coveitise of here skynnes.'
'Artow manlyche amonge thi neighbores · of thi mete
    and drynke?'   260
'I am holden,' quod he, 'as hende · as hounde is in
    kychyne,
Amonges my neighbores, namelich, · such a name ich have.'
'Now God lene nevre,' quod Repentance, · 'but thow
    repent the rather,
The grace on this grounde · thi good wel to bisette,
Ne thine ysue after the · have joye of that thow wynnest, 265
Ne thi executours wel bisett · the silver that thow hem levest;
And that was wonne with wronge · with wikked men be
    despended.
For were I frere of that hous · there gode faith and charite is,
I nolde cope us with thi catel · ne owre kyrke amende,
Ne have a peny to my pitaunce · of thyne, bi my soule
    hele,   270
For the best boke in owre hous · theighe brent golde were the
    leves,
And I wyst wytterly · thow were suche as thow tellest,
Or elles that I kouthe knowe it · by any kynnes wise.
Seruus es alterius · cum fercula pinguia queris,
Pane tuo pocius · vescere, liber eris.   275
    Thow art an unkynde creature, · I can the noughte assoille,
Til thow make restitucioun · and rekne with hem alle,
And sithen that Resoun rolle it · in the regystre of Hevene,
That thow hast made uche man good · I may the noughte
    assoille;
        Non dimittitur peccatum · donec restituatur ablatum,
            &c.
For alle that have of thi good, · have God my trouthe!   280

274-5: You are the slave of another, when you seek after dainty
dishes; feed rather upon bread of your own, and you shall be free.
279: Sin is not remitted, until the theft has been made good.

Ben holden at the heighe dome · to helpe the to restitue.
And who so leveth noughte this be soth · loke in the sauter
     glose,
In *miserere mei deus* · where I mene treuthe,
     Ecce enim veritatem dilexisti, &c.,
     Shal nevere werkman in this worlde · thryve wyth that
          thow wynnest;
Cum sancto sanctus eris, · construe me that on Englische.'   285
     Thanne wex that shrewe in wanhope · and walde have
          hanged him-self,
Ne hadde Repentaunce the rather · reconforted hym in this
     manere,
'Have mercye in thi mynde · and with thi mouth biseche it,
For Goddes mercye is more · than alle hise other werkes;
     Misericordia eius super omnia opera eius, &c.
And al the wikkednesse in this worlde · that man
     myghte worche or thynke,   290
Ne is no more to the mercye of God · than in the see a glede;
     Omnis iniquitas quantum ad misericordiam dei,
     est quasi sintilla in medio maris.
     For-thi have mercy in thi mynde · and marchandise, leve
          it,
For thow hast no good grounde · to gete the with a wastel,
But if it were with thi tonge · or ellis with thi two hondes,
For the good that thow hast geten · bigan al with false-
     hede,   295
And as longe as thow lyvest ther-with · thow yeldest noughte,
     but borwest.
     And if thow wite nevere to whiche · ne whom to restitue,
Bere it to the bisschop · and bidde hym of his grace,
Bisette it hym-selve · as best is for thi soule.

282: 'Look in the commentary on "Have mercy upon me, O God"
[Psalm li] where I truly mean "For behold you have delighted in truth
etc." '
    285: Thou shalt be blessed with the Blessed One.
    290: His mercy is above all his works, etc.
    291: All evil compared with the mercy of God, is like a spark in the
middle of the sea.

D

For he shal answere for the · at the Heygh Dome,   300
For the and for many mo · that man shal yif a rekenynge,
What he lerned yow in Lente · leve thow none other,
And what he lent yow of Owre Lordes good · to lette yow fro
    synne.'

GULA

Now bigynneth Glotoun · for to go to schrifte,
And kaires hym to-kirke-ward · his coupe to schewe.   305
  Ac Beton the brewestere · bad hym good morwe,
And axed of hym with that · whiderward he wolde.
  'To holi cherche,' quod he, · 'forto here masse,
And sithen I wil be shryven · and synne namore.'
  'I have gode ale, gossib,' quod she, · 'Glotown, wiltow
    assaye?'   310
'Hastow aughte in thi purs · any hote spices?'
  'I have peper and piones,' quod she, · 'and a pounde of
    garlike,
A ferthyngworth of fenel-seed · for fastyngdayes.'
  Thanne goth Glotoun in, · and grete othes after;
Cesse the souteresse · sat on the benche,   315
Watte the warner · and his wyf bothe,
Tymme the tynkere · and tweyne of his prentis,
Hikke the hakeneyman · and Hughe the nedeler,
Clarice of Cokkeslane · and the clerke of the cherche,
Dawe the dykere · and a dozeine other;   320
Sire Piers of Pridie · and Peronelle of Flaundres,

A ribibour, a ratonere · a rakyer of Chepe,
A ropere, a redyngkyng · and Rose the dissheres,
Godfrey of Garlekehithe · and Gryfin the Walshe,
And upholderes an hepe, · erly bi the morwe   325
Geven Glotoun with glad chere · good ale to hansel.
    Clement the cobelere · cast of his cloke,
And atte new faire · he nempned it to selle;
Hikke the hakeneyman · hitte his hood after,
And badde Bette the bochere · ben on his side.   330
There were chapmen y-chose · this chaffare to preise;
Who-so haveth the hood · shuld have amendes of the cloke.
    Two risen up in rape · and rouned togideres,
And preised these penyworthes · apart bi hem-selve;
Thei couth noughte bi her conscience · acorden in
        treuthe,   335
Tyl Robyn the ropere · arose by the southe,
And nempned hym for a noumpere · that no debate nere,
For to trye this chaffare · bitwixen hem thre.
    Hikke the hostellere · hadde the cloke,
In covenaunte that Clement · shulde the cuppe fille,   340
And have Hikkes hode hostellere · and holde hym yserved;
And who-so repented rathest · shulde arise after,
And grete Sire Glotoun · with a galoun ale.
    There was laughyng and louryng · and 'let go the cuppe',
And seten so til evensonge · and songen umwhile,   345
Tyl Glotoun had y-globbed · a galoun an a gille.
His guttis gunne to gothely · as two gredy sowes;
He pissed a potel · in a *pater-noster* while,
And blew his rounde ruwet · at his rigge-bon ende,
That alle that herde that horne · held her nose after, 350
And wissheden it had be wexed · with a wispe of firses.
    He myghte neither steppe ne stonde · er he his staffe hadde;
And thanne gan he go · liche a glewmannes bicche,
Somme tyme aside · and somme tyme arrere,
As who-so leyth lynes · forto lacche foules.   355

348: Lord's Prayer.

And whan he drowgh to the dore · thanne dymmed his
  eighen,
He stumbled on the thresshewolde · an threwe to the erthe.
Clement the cobelere · caughte hym bi the myddel,
For to lifte hym alofte · and leyde him on his knowes;
Ac Glotoun was a gret cherle · and a grym in the liftynge,
And coughed up a caudel · in Clementis lappe;   361
Is non so hungri hounde · in Hertford schire
Durst lape of the levynges, · so unlovely thei smaughte.

With al the wo of this worlde · his wyf and his wenche
Baren hym home to his bedde, · and broughte hym therinne.
And after al this excesse · he had an accidie,   366
That he slepe Saterday and Sonday · til sonne yede to reste.
Thanne waked he of his wynkyng · and wiped his eyghen;
The fyrste worde that he warpe · was, 'where is the bolle?'
His wif gan edwite hym tho · how wikkedlich he lyved,   370
And Repentance righte so · rebuked hym that tyme:

'As thow with wordes and werkes · hast wroughte yvel in
  thi lyve,
Shryve the and be shamed ther-of · and shewe it with thi
  mouth.'

'I, Glotoun,' quod the gome, · 'gylti me yelde,
That I have trespassed with my tonge, · I can noughte telle
  how ofte,   375
Sworen "Goddes soule" · and "so God me help and
  halidom,"
There no nede ne was · nyne hundreth tymes;
  And over-seye me at my sopere, · and some tyme at nones,
That I, Glotoun, girt it up · er I hadde gone a myle,
And y-spilte that myghte be spared · and spended on
  somme hungrie: 380
Overdelicatly on fastyng dayes · drunken and eten bothe,
And sat some tyme so longe there · that I slepe and ete at ones.
For love of tales in tavernes · to drynke the more, I dyned,
And hyed to the mete er none · whan fastyng-dayes were.'

'This shewyng shrifte,' quod Repentance, · 'shal be
  meryte to the.'   385

And thanne gan Glotoun grete · and gret doel to make
For his lither lyf · that he lyved hadde,
And avowed to fast — · 'for hunger or for thurst
Shal nevere fisshe on the Fryday · defien in my wombe,
Tyl Abstinence myn aunte · have yive me leve;   390
And yit have I hated hir · al my lyf tyme.'

Thanne come Sleuthe al bislabered · with two slymy
     eighen,
'I most sitte,' seyde the segge, · 'or elles shulde I nappe;
I may noughte stonde ne stoupe · ne with-oute a stole knele.
Were I broughte abedde · but if my taille-ende it made,   395
Sholde no ryngynge do me ryse · ar I were rype to dyne.'

He bygan *benedicite* with a bolke · and his brest knocked,
And roxed and rored · and rutte atte laste.
'What! awake, renke!' quod Repentance, · 'and rape the to
    shrifte.'
  'If I shulde deye bi this day, · me liste noughte to loke; 400
I can noughte perfitly my *pater-noster* · as the prest it
    syngeth,
But I can rymes of Robyn Hood · and Randolf Erle of
    Chestre,
Ac neither of Owre Lorde ne of Owre Lady · the leste that
    evere was made.
  I have made vowes fourty, · and foryete hem on the
    morne;
I parfourned nevre penaunce · as the prest me highte, 405
Ne ryghte sori for my synnes · yet was I nevere.
And yif I bidde any bedes, · but if it be in wrath,
That I telle with my tonge · is two myle fro myne herte.
I am occupied eche day, · haliday and other,
With ydel tales atte ale · and otherwhile in cherches; 410
Goddes peyne and his passioun · ful selde thynke I there-on.
  I visited nevere fieble men · ne fettered folke in puttes,
I have levere here an harlotrie · or a somer game of souteres,
Or lesynges to laughe at · and belye my neighbore,
Than al that evere Marke made, · Mathew, John and
    Lucas. 415
And vigilies and fastyng dayes · alle thise late I passe,
And ligge abedde in Lenten, · an my lemman in myn armes,
Tyl matynes and masse be do, · and thanne go to the freres;
Come I to *ite, missa est* · I holde me yserved.
I nam noughte shryven some tyme, · but if sekenesse it
    make, 420
Nought tweies in two yere, · and thanne up gesse I schryve
    me.
  I have be prest and parsoun · passynge thretti wynter,
Yete can I neither solfe ne synge · ne seyntes lyves rede,

397: Blessed [be the Lord God of Israel . . .].
401: Lord's Prayer.   419: Go, it has been sent.

But I can fynde in a felde · or in a fourlonge an hare,
Better than in *beatus vir* · or in *beati omnes*   425
Construe oon clause wel · and kenne it to my parochienes.
I can holde lovedayes · and here a reves rekenynge,
Ac in canoun ne in the decretales · I can noughte rede a lyne.
   Yif I bigge and borwe it, · but yif it be ytailled,
I foryete it as yerne, · and yif men me it axe   430
Sixe sithes or sevene · I forsake it with othes,
And thus tene I trewe men · ten hundreth tymes.
   And my servaunts some tyme · her salarye is bihynde,
Reuthe is to here the rekenynge · whan we shal rede
      acomptes;
So with wikked wille and wraththe · my werkmen I paye.   435
   Yif any man doth me a benfait · or helpeth me at nede,
I am unkynde agein his curteisye · and can noughte under-
      stonde it;
For I have and have hadde · some dele haukes maneres,
I nam noughte lured with love · but there ligge aughte under
      the thombe.
   The kyndenesse that myne evene-cristene · kidde me
      fernyere,   440
Sixty sythes I, Sleuthe, · have foryete it sith,
In speche and in sparynge of speche · yspilte many a tyme
Bothe flesche and fissche · and many other vitailles;
Bothe bred and ale, · butter, melke, and chese
Forsleuthed in my servyse · til it myghte serve noman.   445
   I ran aboute in youthe · and yaf me noughte to lerne,
And evere sith have be beggere · for my foule sleuthe;
Heu michi, quod sterilem vitam duxi iuuenilem.'
   'Repentestow the naughte?' quod Repentance, · and righte
      with that he swowned,
Til *vigilate* the veille · fette water at his eyghen,   450
And flatte it on his face · and faste on hym criede,

425: Blessed is the man. . . .
      Blessed are all they. . . .
448: Alas, what a barren youthful life I have led!
450: Watch ye!

And seide, 'ware the fram wanhope · wolde the bitraye.
"I am sori for my synnes" · sey so to thi-selve,
And bete thi-selve on the breste · and bidde Hym of grace;
For is no gult here so grete · that His goodnesse nys more.'

Thanne sat Sleuthe up, · and seyned hym swithe,   456
And made avowe to-fore God · for his foule sleuthe,
'Shal no Sondaye be this sevene yere, · but sykenesse it lette,
That I ne shal do me er day · to the dere cherche,
And heren matines and masse, · as I a monke were.   460
Shal none ale after mete · holde me thennes,
Tyl I have evensonge herde, · I behote to the Rode.
And yete wil I yelde agein, · if I so moche have,
Al that I wikkedly wan · sithen I wytte hadde.

And though my liflode lakke · leten I nelle,   465
That eche man ne shal have his · ar I hennes wende:
And with the residue and the remenaunt, · bi the Rode of
       Chestre!
I shal seke Treuthe arst, · ar I se Rome!'

Robert the robbere · on *reddite* lokede,   469
And, for ther was nought wher-of, · he wepe swithe sore.
Ac yet the synful shrewe · seyde to hym-selve,
'Cryst, that on Calvarye · uppon the crosse deydest,
Tho Dismas my brother · bisoughte yow of grace,
And haddest mercy on that man · for *memento* sake,
So rewe on this robbere · that *reddere* ne have,   475
Ne nevere wene to wynne · with crafte that I owe.
But for thi mykel mercy · mitigacioun I biseche;
Ne dampne me noughte at domesday · for that I did so ille.'

What bifel of this feloun · I can noughte faire schewe,
Wel I wote he wepte faste · water with bothe his eyen,   480
And knowleched his gult · to Cryst yete eftsones,
That *penitencia* his pyke · he shulde polsche newe,
And lepe with hym over londe · al his lyf tyme,

469: Render [to all men their dues].   474: Remember [me].
475: Who have not the means to make restitution.
482: penitence.

For he had leyne bi *latro* · Luciferes aunte.

  And thanne had Repentaunce reuthe, · and redde
    hem alle to knele,   485
'For I shal biseche for al synful · owre Saveoure of grace,
To amende us of owre mysdedes · and do mercy to us alle.

  Now God,' quod he, 'that of thi goodnesse · gonne the
    worlde make,
And of naughte madest aughte · and man moste liche to
    thi-selve,
And sithen suffredest for to synne · a sikenesse to us alle, 490
And al for the best, as I bileve, · what ever the boke telleth,

    O felix culpa! o necessarium peccatum ade! &c.

For thourgh that synne thi Sone · sent was to this erthe,
And bicam man of a mayde, · mankynde to save,
And madest thi-self with thi Sone · and us synful yliche,

    Faciamus hominem ad ymaginem et similitudinem
        nostram;
    Et alibi: qui manet in caritate, in deo manet,
      & deus in eo;

  And sith with thi self Sone · in owre sute deydest   495
On Godefryday for mannes sake, · at ful tyme of the daye,
There thi-selfe ne thi Sone · no sorwe in deth feledest;
But in owre secte was the sorwe, · and thi Sone it ladde,

    Captiuam duxit captiuitatem.

  The sonne for sorwe ther-of · les syghte for a tyme
Aboute mydday whan most lighte is · and mele tyme of
    seintes;   500
Feddest with thi fresche blode · owre forfadres in derknesse,

    Populus qui ambulabat in tenebris, vidit lucem
      magnam;

And thorw the lighte that lepe oute of the · Lucifer was
    blent,

484: robber.

491: O happy fault! O necessary sin of Adam! etc.

494: Let us make man in our own image and likeness; And in another text: 'He who dwells in love, dwells in God, and God in him.'

498: He led captivity captive.

501: The people that walked in darkness have seen a great light.

And blewe alle thi blissed · in-to the blisse of Paradise.
  The thrydde daye after · thow yedest in owre sute,
A synful Marie the seighe · ar seynte Marie the dame,   505
And al to solace synful · thow suffredest it so were:
      Non veni vocare iustos, set peccatores ad peni-
          tenciam.
  And al that Marke hath ymade, · Mathew, Johan, and
      Lucas,
Of thyne doughtiest dedes · were don in owre armes.
      Verbum caro factum est, et habitauit in nobis.
And bi so moche, me semeth, · the sikerere we mowe
Bydde and biseche, · if it be thi wille,   510
That art owre fader and owre brother · be merciable to us,
And have reuthe on thise Ribaudes · that repente hem here
      sore,
That evere thei wratthed the in this worlde, · in worde,
      thoughte, or dedes.'
  Thanne hent Hope an horne · of *deus, tu conuersus viuificabis*
      nos,
And blew it with *Beati quorum* · *remisse sunt iniquitates,*   515
That alle seyntes in hevene · songen at ones,
      Homines & iumenta saluabis, quemadmodum
          multiplicasti misericordiam tuam, deus, &c.
A thousand of men tho · thrungen togyderes;
Criede upward to Cryst · and to his clene moder
To have grace to go with hem · Treuthe to seke.
  Ac there was wyghte non so wys · the wey thider
      couthe,   520
But blustreden forth as bestes · over bankes and hilles,
Til late was and longe · that thei a lede mette,
Apparailled as a paynym · in pylgrymes wyse.
He bare a burdoun ybounde · with a brode liste,

506: I came not to call the righteous but sinners to repentance.
508: The word was made flesh, and dwelt among us.
514: You will turn, O God, and bring us to life.
515: Blessed are they whose sins are forgiven.
516: You will preserve men and beasts, O how
      you have multiplied your mercy, O God, etc.

In a withewyndes wise · ywounden aboute.   525
A bolle and a bagge · he bare by his syde;
An hundreth of ampulles · on his hatt seten,
Signes of Synay · and shelles of Galice;
And many a cruche on his cloke · and keyes of Rome,
And the vernicle bifore · for men shulde knowe,   530
And se bi his signes · whom he soughte hadde.
    This folke frayned hym firste · fro whennes he come.
    'Fram Synay,' he seyde, · 'and fram Owre Lordes
        sepulcre;
In Bethleem and in Babiloyne · I have ben in bothe,
In Ermonye, in Alisaundre, · in many other places.   535
Ye may se bi my signes · that sitten on myn hatte,
That I have walked ful wyde · in wete and in drye,
And soughte gode seyntes · for my soules helth.'
    'Knowestow oughte a corseint · that men calle Treuthe?
Coudestow aughte wissen us the weye · where that wy
        dwelleth?'   540
    'Nay, so me God helpe!' · seide the gome thanne,
'I seygh nevere palmere · with pike ne with scrippe
Axen after hym er, · til now in this place.'
'Peter!' quod a plowman, · and put forth his hed,
'I knowe hym as kyndely · as clerke doth his bokes;   545
Conscience and Kynde Witte · kenned me to his place,
And deden me suren hym sikerly · to serve hym for evere,
Both to sowe and to sette · the while I swynke myghte.
I have ben his folwar · al this fifty wyntre;
Bothe ysowen his sede · and sued his bestes,   550
With-inne and with-outen · wayted his profyt.
I dyke and I delve · I do that Treuthe hoteth;
Some tyme I sowe · and some tyme I thresche,
In tailoures crafte and tynkares crafte · what Treuthe can
        devyse,
I weve an I wynde · and do what Treuthe hoteth.   555
    For, thoughe I seye it my-self, · I serve hym to paye;
Ich have myn huire of hym wel · and otherwhiles more;
He is the prestest payer · that pore men knoweth;

He ne with-halt non hewe his hyre · that he ne hath it at even.
He is as low as a lombe · and loveliche of speche,   560
And yif ye wilneth to wite · where that he dwelleth,
I shal wisse yow witterly · the weye to his place.'
　'Ye, leve Pieres,' quod this pilgrymes, · and profered hym
　　huire
For to wende with hem · to Treuthes dwellyng place.
　'Nay, bi my soules helth,' quod Pieres, · and gan forto
　　swere,   565
'I nolde fange a ferthynge · for Seynt Thomas shryne!
Treuthe wolde love me the lasse · a longe tyme thereafter!

*　　*　　*　　*　　*

　Ac there aren sevene sustren · that serven Treuthe evere,
And aren porteres of the posternes · that to the place longeth.
That one hat Abstenence · and Humilite an other,   570
Charite and Chastite · ben his chief maydenes,
Pacience and Pees · moche poeple thei helpeth,
Largenesse the lady · heo let in ful manye;
Heo hath hulpe a thousande oute · of the develes ponfolde.
　And who is sibbe to this sevene, · so me God helpe!   575
He is wonderliche welcome · and faire underfongen.
And but if ye be syb · to summe of thise sevene,
It is ful harde bi myne heved,' quod Peres, · 'for any of yow
　alle
To geten ingonge at any gate there, · but grace be the more.'
　'Now, bi Cryst,' quod a cutpurs, · 'I have no kynne
　　there!'   580
'Ne I,' quod an apewarde, · 'bi aughte that I knowe!'
　'Wite God,' quod a wafrestre, · 'wist I this for sothe,
Shulde I nevere ferthere a fote · for no freres prechynge.'
　'Yus,' quod Pieres the plowman, · and pukked hem alle to
　　gode,
'Mercy is a maydene there · hath myghte ouer hem alle;   585
And she is syb to alle synful, · and her Sone also;
And thorughe the helpe of hem two · (hope thow none other)
Thow myghte gete grace there · bi so thow go bityme.'

'By Seynt Poule,' quod a pardonere, · 'peraventure I be
    noughte knowe there,
I wil go fecche my box with my brevettes · and a bulle with
    bisshopes lettres!'   590
'By Cryst,' quod a comune womman, · 'thi companye
    wil I folwe
Thow shalt sey I am thi sustre, · I ne wot where thei bicome.'

'THIS WERE a wikked way · but who-so hadde a gyde
    That wolde folwen us eche a fote;' · thus this folke hem
      mened.
Quats Perkyn the plouman, · 'bi Seynt Peter of Rome,   595
I have an half acre to erye · bi the heighe way;
Hadde I eried this half acre · and sowen it after,
I wolde wende with yow · and the way teche.'
    'This were a longe lettynge,' · quod a lady in a sklayre,
'What sholde we wommen · worche there-whiles?'   600
'Somme shal sowe the sakke,' quod Piers, · 'for shedyng
    of the whete;
And ye, lovely ladyes · with youre longe fyngres,
That ye han silke and sendal · to sowe, whan tyme is,
Chesibles for chapelleynes · cherches to honoure.
    Wyves and wydwes, · wolle and flex spynneth,   605

Maketh cloth, I conseille yow, · and kenneth so yowre
    doughtres;
The nedy and the naked, · nymmeth hede how hij liggeth,
And casteth hem clothes · for so comaundeth Treuthe.
For I shal lene hem lyflode, · but yif the londe faille,
Flesshe and bred bothe · to riche and to pore,   610
As longe as I lyve · for the Lordes love of hevene.
    And alle manere of men · that thorw mete and drynke
    lybbeth,
Helpith hym to worche wightliche · that wynneth yowre
    fode.'
    'Bi Crist,' quod a knyghte tho, · 'he kenneth us the best;
Ac on the teme trewly · taughte was I nevere.   615
Ac kenne me,' quod the knyghte, · 'and, bi Cryst, I wil
    assaye!'
    'Bi Seynt Poule,' quod Perkyn, · 'ye profre yow so faire,
That I shal swynke and swete · and sowe for us bothe,
And other laboures do for thi love · al my lyf tyme,
In covenaunt that thow kepe · holikirke and my-selve   620
Fro wastoures and fro wykked men · that this worlde
    struyeth.
    And go hunte hardiliche · to hares and to foxes,
To bores and to brockes · that breketh adown myne hegges,
And go affaite the faucones · wilde foules to kille;
For suche cometh to my croft · and croppeth my whete.' 625
    Curteislich the knyghte thanne · comsed thise wordes,
'By my power, Pieres,' quod he, · 'I plighte the my treuthe
To fulfille this forward, · thowgh I fighte sholde;
Als longe as I lyve · I shal the mayntene.'

SECTION III

Easter Week and the Harrowing of Hell

Passus XVI–XVIII

SECTION III

Easter Week and the Harrowing of Hell

Let your loins be girded about, and your lights burning; and
ye yourselves like unto men that wait for their lord, when he
will return from the wedding; that when he cometh and
knocketh, they may open unto him immediately.

The Gospel According to St. Luke, Chapter xii

THERE has been a great deal of scholarly work on the subject of
the story of Christ's descent to Hell on Easter Saturday to release
the souls of the dead from Satan's bondage. There is probably a
suggestion of the idea in pre-Christian Biblical writings, for
example the xxiii Psalm *Attollite Portas*;[1] and Babylonian,
Egyptian, Greek and Persian accounts of descent to the Underworld may well have had their influence. An important New
Testament passage which became a popular text for medieval
preachers was the story from the *First Epistle of S. Peter* (ch. iii,
vv. 18, 19):[2] 'Being put to death in the flesh, but quickened in the
spirit; in which also he went and preached to the souls in prison,
which aforetimes were disobedient, when the longsuffering of
God waited in the days of Noah.'

The fourth Formula of Sirmium (A.D. 359) introduced the
passage 'He descended into Hell' into the Apostles' Creed.[3] The
fully developed account of the Harrowing of Hell — an account
which had immense influence on medieval English literature —
was the apocryphal *Gospel of Nicodemus*, written in the second
or third century. By the tenth century the *Gospel of Nicodemus*
had spread its influence to all Christian artistic production — a
particularly prominent place being accorded to the story of the
blind knight Longinus. The peak of its popularity was reached

[1] xxiv (A.V.)   [2] v. 19 (A.V.)

[3] '. . . the first credal appearance of the Descent to Hell was in the
Fourth Formula of Sirmium, the Dated Creed of 359, which affirmed
(with an allusion to Job 38, 17) that the Lord had "died, and descended
to the underworld, and regulated things there, Whom the gatekeepers
of hell saw and shuddered".' J. N. D. Kelly, *Early Christian Creeds*
(see particularly pp. 378–83).

E

in the dramatic writings of England in the thirteenth and four-teenth centuries. The *Gospel of Nicodemus* was paraphrased in its entirety in the poem, well-known in its time, *Cursor Mundi* which was written in the early fourteenth century. But it was chiefly popularized by the version which appeared in the *Legenda Aurea* (*Golden Legend*), a medieval compilation of ecclesiastical lore. This was very probably the version which Langland used. It is some evidence of its lasting fame when one considers that, a hundred years after *Piers Plowman*, Caxton's publication of the *Golden Legend* was his most popular production.

Stories that originate from the *Gospel of Nicodemus* include those of St. Veronica's handkerchief, Longinus, Antichrist, and Seth's mission to Paradise for the Oil of Mercy and the apple-seeds from which the Holy Rood — the Cross of Calvary — was believed to have sprung.[1]

Though Langland probably knew the *Legenda Aurea*, he and his readers were also acquainted with the story of the Harrowing through the many Mystery plays which incorporated the episode and through the liturgical plays — the earliest form of English drama, in which the clergy enacted Biblical stories, particularly during the great festivals of Christmas and Easter. Sometimes these 'plays' would last only for a few moments in the service; at others, the drama would be more lengthy and impressive. The liturgical play with direct relevance to the present section from *Piers Plowman* is described by E. K. Chambers:[2]

'Take, for example, the ritual, of Gallican origin, used at the dedication of a church. The bishop and his procession approach the closed doors of the church from without, but one of the clergy, *quasi latens*, is placed inside. Three blows with a staff are given on the doors, and the anthem is raised *Tollite portas, principes, vestras et elevamini, portae aeternales, et introibit Rex gloriae*. From within comes the question *Quis est iste Rex gloriae?* and the reply is given *Dominus virtutum ipse est Rex gloriae*. Then the doors are opened, and as the procession sweeps through, he who was concealed within slips out, *quasi fugiens*, to join the train. It is a dramatic expulsion of the spirit of evil. A number of other instances are furnished by the

---

[1] See W. H. Hulme, *The Middle English Harrowing of Hell and Gospel of Nicodemus Now first printed from all the known MSS.*

[2] *The Medieval Stage*, vol. 2, pp. 4–5.

elaborate rites of Holy Week. Thus on Palm Sunday, in commemoration of the entry into Jerusalem, the usual procession before Mass was extended, and went outside the church and round the church-yard or close bearing palms, or in their places sprigs of yew, box, or withies, which the priest had already blessed. The introduction of a *Palmesel* [Palm Sunday ass] might make the ceremony more dramatic still. Some of the texts used were of a prophetic character, and the singer of these was occasionally dressed as a prophet. At the doors of the church the procession was greeted by boys stationed upon the roof of the porch, and certain French uses transferred to the occasion the dedication solemnity of the *Tollite portas* just described.'

In the present *Piers Plowman* passage, we can see how Langland has worked many of these details into the scheme of his poem — the dreamer's meeting with the prophets; the children with palms; the expulsion of the Devil from the church (and, allegorically, because each of us is Mancastle, from the individual); the tropes — all these would be familiar to his audience both from liturgical plays and from their developments in the Mystery plays.

Anyone familiar with the modern Roman Catholic services during Holy Week (which are substantially the same as those of Langland's day) will recognize that Section III follows closely the liturgical usage. The Dreamer states this explicitly, of course. During the last three days of Holy Week the church lights are gradually extinguished, and it is finally left in total darkness; Matins and Lauds on those days are called the 'Tenebrae'. The services of Holy Saturday used to be held during the night vigil between that day and Easter Day. Part of that impressive service was the entry of the paschal candle, the Lumen Christi, into the darkened church. The service continued until daybreak, and at dawn the Easter bells rang forth triumphantly:

> Tyl the daye dawed · this damaiseles daunced,
> That men rongen to the resurexioun.

To Langland, then, the service has two special significances: not only does the congregation represent the Church in mourning, lamenting in darkness the departed Lord; it represents also the souls of all those in the thraldom of Satan, whom the victorious and glorified Light of the World restores to His peace.[1]

The lasting hold of the incident of the Harrowing of Hell in drama can be seen in the strange scene of the Hell-gate Porter in *Macbeth*.[2] Only after repeated knocking at the gate will the porter undo the bolts, though he in fact assumes that he is letting in another soul for the everlasting bonfire. It is Macbeth ('Not in the legions of horrid Hell can come a devil more damn'd in evils') who is appalled by the noise and who fears that the one who knocks at the gates will bring judgement in his wake. Macduff, the Christ-figure, is allowed into the castle after the porter has asked 'Who's there?' (*Quis est iste rex gloriae?*) and, as we might expect, he asks the question 'i' th' name of Belzebub'. At length Macbeth and Macduff fight in single combat, and Macduff emerges victorious. The parallel cannot be carried too far, but there can be no doubt that the Harrowing theme accounts for much of the basic pattern of the passage and a great deal of the imagery.

The immense influence of the *Gospel of Nicodemus* on the creative dramatic imagination of the fourteenth century can hardly be overemphasized; and its effects — and the difficulties in trying to determine whether influence is primary or secondary through some other work — are thus described by Professor Hardin Craig:[3]

'With the next expansion that appears in the York-Towneley plays, certainly in the 14th Century, we have the introduction of the New Testament apocrypha in the use by a reviser of certain plays of the *Gospel of Nicodemus*. . . . The apocryphal gospels in the Middle Ages might be described as sacred writings, and from no point of view can they be regarded as inconsiderable. With their ecclesiastical sanction and their vivid and earnest presentation of realistic and yet marvellous detail they offered a safe and interesting ground for the amplification of the mystery plays ready no doubt to advance beyond the limits of the liturgy. . . . Of these writings the *Gospel*

[1] There is a succinct discussion of the Holy Week services in the introduction, by Adrian Fortescue, to *The Holy Week Book*.

[2] I have already remarked on the castle symbols in that play: see note on line 11 in Section I.

[3] *English Religious Drama of the Middle Ages*, pp. 155-7.

of Nicodemus is the most picturesque and was the most popular. . . . The *Gospel of Nicodemus* was one of the most popular
works of the whole Middle Ages, and it is impossible to be too
positive about it . . . as the immediate source of a particular
work, for there attached to the *Gospel of Nicodemus* a large
body of subordinate apocrypha. . . . The greatest body of
Middle English literature is devoted to the presentation in
English poetry or prose of the great mass of medieval Latin
religious literature. One has to remind oneself that the story of
man's creation, fall and redemption with its multifarious
complications was *the* medieval subject and that it was common
property.'

Langland's Dreamer falls asleep, he tells us, on Palm Sunday,
and, in his dreams during Holy Week, reminiscences from the
service, from his religious reading, from religious drama, from his
own incessant spiritual questioning, become fused into a magnificent poem. All his wanderings in the search for St. Truth and for
an understanding of the justice of God cease at the sight of the
suffering Lord: he has found St. Truth, Justice and Mercy, and,
at last, Peace:

> *Misericordia & veritas obuiauerunt sibi, iusticia & pax*
> *osculate sunt.*

At that point the church bells wake him; and they are the bells
proclaiming the risen Christ.

In the introduction to this edition I remarked that the matter
of great poetry is more weighty than that of a prose translation.
Passus XVIII of *Piers Plowman* communicates on a high and
intense plane which the less ordered medium of prose rarely
reaches. Though the effect is most felt in a reading of the entire
passage, nevertheless even the last line of the passus exemplifies
this:

> 'May no grysly gost · glyde there it shadweth!'

Here the overtones of horror of the preceding events are reflected
in the eeriness of *glyde* and in the three-stressed *g*'s; but the
release from the central tension of the alliterative line reflects the
Dreamer's new-found peace, and the final stress falls on the soft
sounds of *shadweth*.

It may be of interest to see the passage from the *Legenda Aurea* which Langland had almost certainly read.[1] In the *Gospel of Nicodemus* it is said that Carinus and Leucius, sons of Simeon, rose with Christ and related the events of the harrowing:

> Cum essemus cum omnibus patribus nostris patriarchis in caligine tenebrarum, subito factus est aureus color purpureusque et regalis lux illustrans super nos, statimque Adam humani generis pater exsultavit. . . . Et exclamauit Ysaias dicens: Haec est lux patris, filius Dei, sicut praedixi, cum essem vivus in terris — populus, qui ambulabat in tenebris, vidit lucem magnam. . . . Post hoc . . . quidam eremi cultor . . . dixit: Ego sum Iohannes, qui Christum baptizavi . . . dicens: Ecce agnus Dei . . . omnes patriarchae et prophetae exsultaverunt . . . [Satan and 'Inferus' discuss this appearance of Christ.] Cui inferus: Ipse ne est qui suscitavit Lazarum, quem tenebam? Cui Sathan: Ipse est . . . facta est vox ut tonitruum dicens: Tollite portas, principes, vestras, et elevamini, portae aeternales; et introibit rex gloriae. Ad hanc vocem concurrerunt daemones et ostia aenea cum vectibus ferreis clauserunt. . . . Facta est iterum vox maxima dicens: Tollite portas, etc. Videns inferus quod duabus vicibus clamaverat, quasi ignorans dixit: Quis est iste rex gloriae?[2]

A comparison of this passage with *Piers Plowman* will leave the reader in little doubt that Langland had the *Legenda Aurea* on his desk or in his memory when he wrote the poem. But the

---

[1] Chapter called 'De Resurrectione Domini' in the *Legenda Aurea* of Jacobus a Varagine.

[2] When we were in gloomy darkness with all our fathers, the patriarchs, suddenly above us there appeared shining a brilliant, golden and royal light. And immediately Adam, the father of the human race, rejoiced . . . and Isaiah cried out saying: 'This is the light of the Father, the Son of God, as I prophesied when I was alive on earth — "The people that walked in darkness have seen a great light." ' . . . After this . . . a certain dweller in the desert . . . said: 'I am John, who baptized Christ . . . saying: "Behold, the Lamb of God." ' . . . All the patriarchs and prophets rejoiced. . . . Inferus replied: 'Is not this he who raised up Lazarus whom I held prisoner?' To whom Satan replied: 'It is he.' . . . Then there was a voice like thunder, which said: 'Raise your gates, ye princes, and be ye lifted up, ye everlasting doors; and the King of Glory shall come in.' At the sound of this voice, the devils ran together, and they closed the brazen gates with iron bolts. . . . Then again the exceedingly powerful voice said: 'Raise the gates, etc.' Inferus, seeing that he had called out on two occasions, feigned ignorance, and said: 'Who is that King of Glory?'

lively writing of the *Legenda Aurea* is transformed by Langland
into poetry whose dignity and intensity take us, as it were, by
surprise. The medieval mystic writers held that the spiritual
significance or clarity of exposition of the religious theme must
never be obscured by the embellishment of poetry.[1] In this
passage Langland pleases all tastes, modern and medieval: the
simple splendour of his words and rhythms raises our minds to
the highest planes of religious experience. The allegorical
meaning of the passage is, of course, that each of us is Satan's
domain in which a soul is imprisoned *in tenebris*, and we can
hardly fail to be simultaneously excited and humiliated by the
majesty of such lines as:

> Dukes of this dym place · anon undo this gates,
> That Cryst may come in · the Kynges Sone of Hevene.

> And I awaked there-with · and wyped myne eyghen,
> And after Piers the plowman · pryed and stared.
> Estwarde and westwarde · I awayted after faste,
> And yede forth as an ydiote · in contre to aspye
> After Pieres the plowman; · many a place I soughte.   5
> And thanne mette I with a man, · a mydlenten Sondaye,
> As hore as an hawethorne, · and Abraham he highte.
> I frayned hym first · fram whennes he come,
> And of whennes he were · and whider that he thoughte.
> 'I am Feith,' quod that freke, · 'it falleth noughte to
> lye,   10
> And of Abrahames hous · an heraud of armes.
> I seke after a segge · that I seigh ones,
> A ful bolde bacheler, · I knewe hym by his blasen.'
> 'What bereth that buirn?' quod I tho, · 'so blisse the
> bityde!'
> 'Thre leodes in o lith, · non lenger than other,   15
> Of one mochel and myghte · in mesure and in lengthe;
> That one doth, alle doth, · and eche doth by his one.
> The firste hath mighte and majestee, · maker of alle thinges;

---

[1] See Elizabeth Salter, *Piers Plowman: An Introduction*, pp. 24–29.

Pater is his propre name, · a persone by hym-selve.
The secounde of that sire is · sothfastnesse, *filius*,   20
Wardeyne of that witte hath, · was evere with-oute gynnynge.
The thridde hatte the holygoost, · a persone by hym-selve,
The lighte of alle that lyf hath · a londe and a watre,
Confortoure of creatures, · of hym cometh al blisse.
So thre bilongeth for a lorde · that lordeship claymeth,   25
Myghte, and a mene · to knowe his owne myghte,
Of hym and of his servaunt · and what thei suffre bothe.
So God that gynnyng hadde nevre · but tho hym good
      thoughte,
Sent forth his Sone · as for servaunt that tyme,
To occupien hym here · til issue were spronge,   30
That is, children of Charite · and Holicherche the moder.
Patriarkes and prophetes · and aposteles were the chyldren,
And Cryst and crystenedome · and crystene holy-cherche.
In menynge that man moste · on o God bileve,
And there Hym lyked and loved · in thre persones Hym
      shewed.'   35

*   *   *   *   *

'And thus I seke Hym,' he seide, · 'for I herde seyne late
Of a barne that baptised Hym, · Johan Baptiste was his name,
That to patriarkes and to prophetes · and to other peple in
      derknesse
Seyde that he seigh here · that sholde save us alle;
      Ecce agnus dei, &c.'
I hadde wonder of his wordes · and of his wyde clothes;   40
For in his bosome he bar a thyng · that he blissed evere.
And I loked on his lappe, · a lazar lay there-inne
Amonges patriarkes and profetes · pleyande togyderes.
'What awaytestow?' quod he. · 'And what woldestow have?'
'I wolde wyte,' quod I tho, · 'what is in yowre lappe.'   45
   'Loo!' quod he, and lete me se. · 'Lorde, mercy!' I seide,
'This is a present of moche prys. · What Prynce shal it have?'

19: The Father.   20: The Son.
39: Behold, the Lamb of God, etc.

'It is a preciouse present,' quod he, · 'ac the pouke it hath
    attached,
And me there-myde,' quod that man, · 'may no wedde us
    quite,
Ne no buyrn be owre borwgh · ne bryng us fram his
    daungere;   50
Oute of the poukes pondfolde · no meynprise may us
    fecche,
Tyl he come that I carpe of, · Cryst is his name,
That shal delyvre us some daye · out of the develes powere,
And better wedde for us legge · than we ben alle worthy,
That is, lyf for lyf, · or ligge thus evere   55
Lollynge in my lappe · tyl such a lorde us fecche.'
    'Allas!' I seyde, 'that synne · so longe shal lette
The myghte of Goddes mercy · that myght us alle
    amende!'
I wepte for his wordes; · with that sawe I an other
Rapelich renne forth; · the righte waye he went.   60
I affrayned hym fyrste · fram whennes he come,
And what he highte and whider he wolde, · and wightlich he
    tolde.
'I am Spes,' quod he, 'a spye, · and spire after a knyghte,
That toke me a maundement · upon the Mounte of Synay,
To reule alle rewmes with; · I bere the writte here.'   65
'Is it asseled?' I seyde. · 'May men se thi lettres?'
'Nay,' he sayde, 'I seke hym · that hath the sele to kepe;
    And that is, crosse and crystenedome · and Cryst there-on
    to hange.
And whan it is asseled so · I wote wel the sothe,
That Lucyferes lordeship · laste shal no lenger.'   70
'Late se thi lettres,' quod I, · 'we mighte the Lawe knowe.'
    Thanne plokked he forth a patent, · a pece of an harde
    roche,
Wher-on were writen two wordes · on this wyse y-glosed,
    Dilige deum & proximum tuum, &c.
This was the tixte trewly, · I toke ful gode yeme;
        73: Love God and your neighbour etc.

The glose was gloriousely writen · with a gilte penne,   75
    In hijs duobus mandatis tota lex pendet & pro-
        phetia.

  'Ben here alle thi lordes lawes?' quod I. · 'Ye leve me wel,'
    he seyde,
'And who so worcheth after this writte · I wil undertaken,
Shal nevere devel hym dere · ne deth in soule greve.
For though I seye it my-self · I have saved with this charme
Of men and of wommen · many score thousandes.'   80
  'He seith soth,' seyde this heraud, · 'I have yfounde it ofte;
Lo here in my lappe · that leved on that charme,
Josue and Judith · and Judas Macabeus,
Ye, and sexty thousande bisyde forth · that ben nought
    seyen here.'
  'Yowre wordes aren wonderful,' quod I tho, ·
    'which of yow is trewest,   85
And lelest to leve on · for lyf and for soule?
Abraham seith that he seigh · Holy the Trinite,
Thre persones in parcelles · departable fro other,
And alle thre but o God, · thus Abraham me taughte,
And hath saved that bileved so · and sory for her synnes,   90
He can noughte segge the somme, · and some aren in his
    lappe,
What neded it thanne · a newe Lawe to bigynne,
Sith the fyrst sufficeth · to savacioun and to blisse?
  And now cometh Spes, and speketh, · that hath aspied
    the Lawe,
And telleth noughte of the Trinitee · that toke hym his
    lettres,   95
"To byleve and lovye · in o Lorde Almyghty,
And sitthe right as my-self · so lovye alle peple."
  The gome that goth with o staf · he semeth in gretter hele
Than he that goth with two staves, · to syghte of us alle.
And righte so, by the Rode! · resoun me sheweth,   100
It is lyghter to lewed men · a lessoun to knowe,
Than for to techen hem two · and to harde to lerne the leest!

75 : On these two commandments hang all the Law and the prophets.

It is ful harde for any man · on Abraham byleve,
And welawey worse yit · for to love a shrewe!
It is lighter to leve · in thre lovely persones   105
Than for to lovye and leve · as wel lorelles as lele.
Go thi gate,' quod I to Spes, · 'so me God helpe!
Tho that lerneth thi lawe · wil litel while usen it!'
And as we wenten thus in the weye, · wordyng togyderes,
Thanne seye we a Samaritan · sittende on a mule,   110
Rydynge ful rapely · the right weye we yeden,
Comynge fro a cuntre · that men called Jerico;
To a justes in Jeherusalem · he chaced awey faste.
Bothe the heraud and Hope · and he mette at ones
Where a man was wounded · and with theves taken.   115
He myghte neither steppe ne stonde · ne stere fote ne handes,
Ne helpe hym-self sothely, · for semivyf he semed,
And as naked as a nedle · and none helpe aboute hym.

    Feith had first sighte of hym, · ac he flegh on syde,
And nolde nought neighen hym · by nyne londes
    lengthe.   120
    Hope cam hippyng after, · that hadde so ybosted,
How he with Moyses maundement · hadde many men
    y-holpe;
Ac whan he hadde sighte of that segge · a-syde he gan hym
    drawe,
Dredfully, by this day! as duk · doth fram the faucoun.
    Ac so sone so the Samaritan · hadde sighte of this lede, 125
He lighte adown of Lyard · and ladde hym in his hande,
And to the wye he went · his woundes to biholde,
And parceyved bi his pous · he was in peril to deye,
And but if he hadde recovrere the rather · that rise shulde
    he nevre;
And breyde to his boteles · and bothe he atamede;   130
Wyth wyn and with oyle · his woundes he wasshed,
Enbawmed hym and bonde his hed · and in his lappe hym
    layde,
And ladde hym so forth on Lyard · to *Lex Christi*, a graunge,
        133: Christ's Law.

Wel six myle or sevene · biside the newe market;
Herberwed hym at an hostrye, · and to the hostellere
    called,   135
And sayde, 'Have, kepe this man · til I come fro the justes,
And lo here sylver,' he seyde, · 'for salve to his woundes.'
And he toke hym two pans, · to lyflode as it were,
And seide, 'What he speneth more, · I make the good
    here-after;
For I may nought lette,' quod that leode; · and Lyarde he
    bistrydeth,   140
And raped hym to-Jherusalem-ward, · the righte waye to
    ryde.
    Faith folweth after faste · and fonded to mete hym,
And Spes spaklich hym spedde, · spede if he myghte,
To overtake hym and talke to hym · ar thei to toun come.
    And whan I seygh this, I sojourned noughte · but shope
    me to renne,   145
And suwed that Samaritan · that was so ful of pite,
And graunted hym to ben his grome. · 'Gramercy,' he seyde,
'Ac thi frende and thi felawe,' quod he, · 'thow fyndest me
    at nede.'
    And I thanked hym tho, · and sith I hym tolde,
How that Feith fleigh awey · and Spes his felaw bothe,   150
For sighte of the sorweful man · that robbed was with
    theves.
    'Have hem excused,' quod he, · 'her help may litel
    availle;
May no medcyn on molde · the man to hele brynge,
Neither Feith ne fyn Hope, · so festred ben his woundis,
Without the blode of a barn · borne of a mayde.   155
And be he bathed in that blode, · baptised, as it were,
And thanne plastred with penaunce · and passioun of that
    babi,
He shulde stonde and steppe; · ac stalworth worth he nevre,
Tyl he have eten al the barn · and his blode ydronke.
For went nevere wy in this worlde · thorw that wilder-
    nesse,   160

That he ne was robbed or rifled, · rode he there or yede,
Save Faith, and his felaw, · Spes, and my-selve,
And thi-self now, and such · as suwen owre werkis.
    For outlawes in the wode · and under banke lotyeth,
And may uch man se · and gode merke take,   165
Who is bihynde and who bifore, · and who ben on hors,
For he halt hym hardyer on horse · than he that is a fote.
For he seigh me, that am Samaritan, · suwen Feith and his
    felaw
On my caple that hatte *Caro*, · of mankynde I toke it,
He was unhardy, that harlot, · and hudde hym *in inferno*   170
Ac ar this day thre dayes, · I dar undertaken,
That he worth fettred, that feloune, · fast with cheynes,
And nevre eft greve grome · that goth this ilke gate;
      O mors, ero mors tua, &c.
    And thanne shal Feith be forester here · and in this fritth
    walke,
And kennen out comune men, · that knoweth noughte the
    contre,   175
Which is the weye that ich went, · and wherforth to
    Jherusalem.
And Hope the hostelleres man shal be · there the man lith
    an helynge;
And alle that fieble and faynt be, · that Faith may nought
    teche,
Hope shal lede hem forth with love, · as his lettre telleth,
And hostel hem and hele · thorw Holicherche bileve,   180
Tyl I have salve for alle syke, · and thanne shal I retourne,
And come agein bi this contree · and confort alle syke
That craveth it or coveiteth it · and cryeth there-after.
For the barne was born in Bethleem · that with his blode
    shal save
Alle that lyveth in Faith and folweth · his felawes
    techynge.'   185
    'A! swete syre!' I seyde tho, · 'wher shal I byleve,

      169: flesh.   170: in Hell.
      173: O death, I shall be thy death, etc.

As Feith and his felawe · enfourmed me bothe?
In thre persones departable · that perpetuel were evere,
And alle thre but o God, · thus Abraham me taughte; —
And Hope afterwarde · he bad me to lovye   190
O God wyth al my good · and alle gomes after,
Lovye hem lyke my-selve, · ac Owre Lorde above alle.'

'After Abraham,' quod he, · 'that heraud of armes,
Sette faste thi faith · and ferme bileve.
And, as Hope highte the, · I hote that thow lovye   195
Thyn evene-crystene evermore · evene forth with thiself.

*   *   *   *   *

For there nys syke ne sori · ne non so moche wrecche,
That he ne may lovye, and hym lyke, · and lene of his herte
Goed wille and good worde · bothe wisshen and willen
Alle manere men · mercy and forgifnesse,   200
And lovye hem liche hym-self, · and his lyf amende. —
I may no lenger lette,' quod he, · and Lyarde he pryked,
And went away as wynde; · and there-with I awaked.

WOLLEWARD and wete-shoed · went I forth after,
  As a reccheles renke · that of no wo reccheth,   205
And yede forth lyke a lorel · al my lyf tyme,
Tyl I wex wery of the worlde, · and wylned eft to slepe,
And lened me to a Lenten · and longe tyme I slepte;
And of Crystes passioun and penaunce · the peple that
  of-raughte,
Reste me there, and rutte faste · tyl *ramis palmarum*;   210
Of gerlis and of *gloria laus* · gretly me dremed,
And how *osanna* by orgonye · olde folke songen.
  One semblable to the Samaritan, · and some del to Piers
    the plowman,
Barfote on an asse bakke · botelees cam prykye,
Wyth-oute spores other spere, · spakliche he loked,   215
As is the kynde of a knyghte · that cometh to be dubbed,
To geten hem gylte spores · or galoches ycouped.
  Thanne was Faith in a fenestre · and cryde '*a! fili David!*'
As doth an heraude of armes · whan auntrous cometh to
    justes.
Olde Juwes of Jerusalem · for joye thei songen,   220
      Benedictus qui venit in nomine domini.
  Thanne I frayned at Faith · what al that fare be-mente,
And who sholde jouste in Jherusalem; · 'Jhesus,' he seyde,
'And fecche that the fende claymeth, · Piers fruit the
    plowman.'
'Is Piers in this place?' quod I, · and he preynte on me,
'This Jhesus of his gentrice · wole juste in Piers armes,   225
In his helme and in his haberjoun, · *humana natura*.
That Cryst be nought biknowe here · for *consummatus deus*,
In Piers paltok the plowman · this priker shal ryde;
For no dynte shal hym dere · as *in deitate patris*.'
'Who shal juste with Jhesus?' quod I, · 'Juwes or
    scribes?'   230

          210: with branches of palms.   211: glory and praise.
          212: Hosanna.   218: O! Son of David!
          220: Blessed is He that comes in the name of the Lord.
          226: human nature.   227: God become man.
          229: in the divine nature of the Father.

'Nay,' quod he, 'the foule fende, · and Fals Dome and
    Deth.
Deth seith he shal fordo · and adown brynge
Al that lyveth or loketh · in londe or in watere.
Lyf seyth that he likth, · and leyth his life to wedde,
That for al that Deth can do · with-in thre dayes,   235
To walke and fecche fro the fende · Piers fruite the plowman,
And legge it there hym lyketh, · and Lucifer bynde,
And forbete and adown brynge · Bale and Deth for evere:
        O mors, ero mors tua!'
Thanne cam Pilatus with moche peple, · *sedens pro tribunali,*
To se how doughtilich Deth sholde do · and deme her
        botheres righte.   240
The Juwes and the justice · ageine Jhesu thei were,
And al her courte on hym cryde · *crucifige* sharpe.
Tho put hym forth a piloure · bifor Pilat, and seyde,
'This Jhesus of owre Jewes temple · japed and dispised,
To fordone it on o day · and in thre dayes after   245
Edefye it eft newe — · here he stant that seyde it —
And yit maken it as moche · in al manere poyntes,
Both as longe and as large · bi loft and by grounde.'
    '*Crucifige*,' quod a cacchepolle, · 'I warante hym a wicche!'
'*Tolle, tolle!*' quod an other, · and toke of kene thornes,   250
And bigan of kene thorne · a gerelande to make,
And sette it sore on his head, · and seyde in envye,
    '*Aue rabby!*' quod that ribaude, · and threw redes at hym,
Nailled hym with thre nailles · naked on the Rode,
And poysoun on a pole · thei put up to his lippes,   255
And bede hym drynke his deth-yvel, · his dayes were ydone.
'And yif that thow sotil be · help now thi-selven,
If thow be Cryst, and kynges sone, · come downe of the
        Rode;
Thanne shul we leve that Lyf the loveth · and will noughte
        lete the deye!'

238: O! death, I shall be thy death!
239: sitting before the judgement seat.   242 and 249: crucify!
250: Away with him!   253: 'Hail, rabbi!'

'*Consummatum est*,' quod Cryst, · and comsed forto
    swowe,   260
Pitousliche and pale · as a prisoun that deyeth;
The Lorde of lyf and of lighte · tho leyed his eyen togideres.
The daye for drede with-drowe · and derke bicam the sonne,
The wal wagged and clef, · and al the worlde quaved.
Ded men for that dyne · come out of depe graves,   265
And tolde whi that tempest · so longe tyme dured.
'For a bitter bataille,' · the ded bodye sayde;
'Lyf and Deth in this derknesse · her one fordoth her other;
Shal no wighte wite witterly · who shal have the maystrye,
Er Sondey aboute sonne rysynge,' · and sank with that til
    erthe.   270
Some seyde that he was Goddes sone, · that so faire deyde,
       Vere filius dei erat iste, &c.
And somme saide he was a wicche, · 'Good is that we assaye,
Where he be ded or noughte ded, · doun er he be taken.'
    Two theves also · tholed deth that tyme,
Uppon a crosse bisydes Cryst, · so was the comune lawe. 275
A cacchepole cam forth · and craked bothe her legges,
And her armes after, · of eyther of tho theves.
Ac was no boy so bolde · Goddes body to touche;
For he was knyghte and kynges sone, · Kynde forgaf that
    tyme,
That non harlot were so hardy · to leyne hande uppon
    hym.   280
    Ac there cam forth a knyghte, · with a kene spere
    ygrounde,
Highte Longeus, as the lettre telleth, · and longe had lore his
    sighte.
Bifor Pilat and other peple · in the place he hoved;
Maugre his many tethe · he was made that tyme
To take the spere in his honde · and justen with Jhesus; 285
For alle thei were unhardy, · that hoved on hors or stode,
To touche hym or to taste hym · or take hym down of Rode.

      260: It is accomplished.
      271: Truly, this man was the Son of God, etc.

F

But this blynde bacheler thanne · bar hym thorugh the
    herte;
The blode spronge down by the spere · and unspered the
    knightes eyen.
Thanne fel the knyghte upon knees, · and cryed hym
    mercy —   290
'Ayeyne my wille it was, lorde, · to wownde yow so sore!'
He seighed and sayde, · 'sore it me athynketh;
For the dede that I have done · I do me in yowre grace;
Have on me reuth, rightful Jhesu!' · and right with that he
    wept.

    Thanne gan Faith felly · the fals Juwes dispise,   295
Called hem caytyves · acursed for evere,
For this foule vyleynye, · 'venjaunce to yow alle,
To do the blynde bete hym ybounde, · it was a boyes
    conseille.
Cursed caytyve! · knighthod was it nevere
To mysdo a ded body · by day or by nyghte.   300
The gree yit hath he geten, · for al his grete wounde.
    For yowre champioun chivaler, · chief knyght of yow alle,
Yelt hym recreaunt rennyng, · right at Jhesus wille.

For be this derkenesse ydo · his deth worth avenged,
And ye, lordeynes, han ylost, · for Lyf shal have the
    maistrye,   305
And yowre fraunchise, that fre was, · fallen is in thraldome,
And ye, cherles, and yowre children, · chieve shal ye nevre,
Ne have lordship in londe · ne no londe tylye,
But al bareyne be · and usurye usen,
Which is lyf that owre Lorde · in alle lawes acurseth.   310
Now yowre good dayes ar done, · as Danyel prophecyed,
Whan Cryst cam, of her kyngdom · the croune shulde
    [cesse];
        Cum veniat sanctus sanctorum, cessabit unxio vestra.'
  What for fere of this ferly · and of the fals Juwes,
I drowe me in that derkenesse · to *decendit ad inferna.*
And there I sawe sothely · *secundum scripturas,*   315
Out of the west coste · a wenche, as me thoughte,
Cam walkynge in the wey, · to-helle-ward she loked.
Mercy hight that mayde, · a meke thynge with-alle,
A ful benynge buirde, · and boxome of speche.
  Her suster, as it semed, · cam softly walkynge,   320
Evene out of the est, · and westward she loked.
A ful comely creature, · Treuth she highte,
For the vertue that hir folwed, · aferd was she nevere.
  Whan this maydenes mette, · Mercy and Treuth,
Eyther axed other · of this grete wonder,   325
Of the dyne and of the derknesse · and how the daye rowed
And which a lighte and a leme · lay befor Helle.
'Ich have ferly of this fare, · in feith,' seyde Treuth,
'And am wendyng to wyte · what this wonder meneth.'
  'Have no merveille,' quod Mercy, · 'myrthe it
    bytokneth.   330
A mayden that hatte Marye, · and moder with-out felyng
Of any kynnes creature, · conceyved thorw speche
And grace of the Holygoste; · wex grete with childe;
With-outen wem · in-to this worlde she brought hym;

312: When the Holy of Holies comes, your anointing will cease.
314: He descended into Hell.   315: according to the scriptures.

And that my tale be trewe, · I take God to witnesse.   335
Sith this barn was bore · ben xxx^{ti} wynter passed;
Which deyde and deth tholed · this day aboute mydday.
And that is cause of this clips · that closeth now the sonne,
In menynge that man shal · fro merkenesse be drawe,
The while this lighte and this leme · shal Lucyfer ablende.
For patriarkes and prophetes · han preched her-of often,   341
That man shal man save · thorw a maydenes helpe,
And that was tynt thorw tre, · tree shal it wynne,
And that deth doun broughte · deth shal releve.'
   'That thow tellest,' quod Treuth, · 'is but a tale of
     waltrot;   345
For Adam and Eve, · and Abraham with other
Patriarkes and prophetes · that in peyne liggen
Leve thow never that yone lighte · hem alofte brynge,
Ne have hem out of Helle; · holde thi tonge, Mercy!
It is but a trufle that thow tellest, · I, Treuth, wote the
     sothe.   350
For that is ones in Helle · out cometh it nevere;
Job the prophete, patriarke, · reproveth thi sawes,
    Quia in inferno nulla est redempcio.'
   Thanne Mercy ful myldly · mouthed thise wordes,
'Thorw experience,' quod she, · 'I hope thei shal be saved.
For venym for-doth venym, · and that I prove by resoun.   355
For of alle venymes · foulest is the scorpioun
May no medcyne helpe · the place there he styngeth,
Tyl he be ded and do ther-to · the yvel he destroyeth,
The fyrst venymouste · thorw venym of hym-self.
So shal this deth for-do, · I dar my lyf legge,   360
Al that deth fordyd furste, · thorw the develles entysynge;
And right as thorw gyle · man was bigyled,
So shal grace that bigan · make a good sleighte;
    Ars vt artem falleret.'
'Now suffre we,' seyde Treuth, · 'I se, as me thinketh,
Out of the nippe of the north, · nought ful fer hennes,   365

    352 : Because in Hell there is no redemption.
    363 : That art might conceal its artifice.

Rightwisnesse come rennynge; · reste we the while;
For he wote more than we, · he was er we bothe.'
　'That is soth,' seyde Mercy. · 'And I se here bi southe,
Where Pees cometh playinge, · in Pacience yclothed;
Love hath coveyted hir longe, · leve I none other　　　370
But he sent hir some lettre · what this lighte bymeneth,
That over-hoveth Helle thus; · she us shal telle.'
　　Whan Pees, in Pacience yclothed, · approched nere hem
　　　tweyne,
Rightwisnesse hir reverenced · for her riche clothyng,
And preyed Pees to telle hir · to what place she wolde,　375
And in her gay garnements · whom she grete thoughte.
　'My wille is to wende,' quod she, · 'and welcome hem alle,
That many day myghte I noughte se, · for merkenesse of
　　　synne,
Adam and Eve · and other moo in Helle.
Moyses and many mo · Mercy shal have,　　　　　　　380
And I shal daunce ther-to, · do thow so, sustre!
For Jhesus justed wel · joye bygynneth dawe;
　　　Ad vesperum demorabitur fletus, & ad matutinum
　　　leticia.
Love, that is my lemman, · suche lettres me sente,
That Mercy, my sustre, and I · mankynde shulde save,
And that God hath forgyven · and graunted me, Pees, and
　　　Mercy,　　　　　　　　　　　　　　　　　　　385
To be mannes meynpernoure · for evere-more after.
Lo! here the patent!' quod Pees, · '*in pace in idipsum* —
And that this dede shal dure — · *dormiam & requiescam.*'
　'What, ravestow?' quod Rightwisnesse, · 'or thow art
　　　right dronke!
Levestow that yonde lighte · unlouke myghte Helle,　　390
And save mannes soule? · sustre, wene it nevre!
At the bygynnynge, God · gaf the dome hym-selve,
That Adam and Eve, · and alle that hem suwed,

382: In the evening weeping shall have place, and in the morning
gladness.
387 and 388: In peace. . . . I shall both sleep and rest.

Shulde deye doune righte · and dwelle in pyne after,
If that thei touched a tre · and the fruite eten.   395
Adam afterward, · ageines his defence,
Frette of that fruit · and forsoke, as it were,
The love of owre Lorde · and his lore bothe,
And folwed that the fende taughte · and his felawes wille,
Ageines resoun; I, Rightwisnesse · recorde thus with
    Treuth,   400
That her peyne be perpetuel · and no preyere hem helpe.
For-thi late hem chewe as thei chose, · and chyde we
    nought, sustres,
For it is botelees bale · the bite that thei eten.'
  'And I shal preve,' quod Pees, · 'her peyne mote
    have ende,
And wo in-to wel · mowe wende atte laste;   405
For had thei wist of no wo, · wel had thei noughte knowen.
For no wighte wote what wel is · that nevere wo suffred,
Ne what is hote hunger · that had nevere defaute.
If no nyghte ne were · no man, as I leve,
Shulde wite witterly · what day is to mene;   410
Shulde nevere righte riche man · that lyveth in reste and ese
Wyte what wo is · ne were the deth of kynde.
So God that bygan al · of his good wille
Bycam man of a mayde · mankynde to save,
And suffred to be solde · to see the sorwe of deyinge,   415
The which unknitteth al kare · and comsynge is of reste.
For til *modicum* mete with us, · I may it wel avowe,
Wote no wighte, as I wene, · what is ynough to mene.
  For-thi God of his goodnesse · the fyrste gome Adam,
Sette hym in solace · and in sovereigne myrthe;   420
And sith he suffred hym synne · sorwe to fele,
To wite what wel was, · kyndelich to knowe it.
And after God auntred Hym-self · and toke Adames kynde,
To wyte what he hath suffred · in thre sondri places,
Bothe in Hevene, and in Erthe · and now til Helle he
    thynketh,   425

417: moderation.

To wite what al wo is · that wote of al joye.

   So it shal fare bi this folke; · her foly and her synne
Shall lere hem what langour is · and lisse with-outen ende.
Wote no wighte what werre is · there that pees regneth,
Ne what is witterly wel · til weyllowey hym teche.'   430

   Thanne was there a wighte · with two brode eyen,
Boke highte that beupere, · a bolde man of speche.
'By Godes body,' quod this Boke, · 'I wil bere witnesse,
That tho this barne was ybore · there blased a sterre,
That alle the wyse of this worlde · in o witte acordeden,   435
That such a barne was borne · in Bethleem Citee,
That mannes soule sholde save · and synne destroye.
And alle the elements,' quod the Boke, · 'her-of bereth
    witnesse,
That he was God that al wroughte, · the walkene firste
    shewed;
Tho that weren in Hevene · token *stella comata*,   440
And tendeden hir as a torche · to reverence His birthe;
The lyghte folwed the Lorde · in-to the lowe erthe.
The water witnessed that He was God, · for he went on it;
Peter the apostle · parceyved His gate,
And as He went on the water · wel hym knewe, and seyde,
    Iube me venire ad te super aquas.
And lo! how the sonne gan louke · her lighte in her-self,   446
Whan she seye Hym suffre · that sonne and se made.
The Erthe for hevynesse · that He wolde suffre,
Quaked as quykke thinge, · and al biquashte the roche.
Lo! Helle mighte noughte holde · but opened tho God
    tholed,   450
And lete oute Symondes sones · to seen hym hange on
    Rode.
And now shal Lucifer leve it, · thowgh hym loth thinke;
For gygas the geaunt · with a gynne engyned
To breke and to bete doune · that ben ageines Jhesus.
'And I, Boke, wil be brent, · but Jhesus rise to lyve,   455
In alle myghtes of man · and his moder gladye,

    440: a comet.   445: Bid me come to you upon the waters.

And conforte al his kynne · and out of care brynge,
And al the Juwen joye · unjoignen and unlouken;
And, but thei reverencen his Rode · and his resurexioun,
And bileve on a Newe Lawe, · be lost lyf and soule.' 460
    'Suffre we,' seide Treuth, · 'I here and se bothe,
How a spirit speketh to Helle, · and bit unspere the gatis,
            Attollite portas, &c.'
A voice loude in that lighte · to Lucifer cryeth,
'Prynces of this place, · unpynneth and unlouketh!
For here cometh with croune · that Kynge is of Glorie.' 465
Thanne syked Sathan, · and seyde to hem alle,
'Suche a lyghte, ageines owre leve, · Lazar it fette;
Care and combraunce · is comen to us alle.
If this kynge come in, · mankynde wil he fecche,
And lede it ther hym lyketh · and lyghtlych me bynde. 470
Patriarkes and prophetes · han parled her-of longe,
That such a lorde and a lyght · shulde lede hem alle
      hennes.'
    'Lysteneth,' quod Lucifer, · 'for I this Lorde knowe,
Bothe this Lorde and this lighte; · is longe ago I knewe
      Hym.
May no deth Hym dere, · ne no develes queyntise, 475
And where He wil is His waye · ac war Hym of the periles;
If He reve me my righte, · He robbeth me by maistrye.
For by right and bi resoun · tho renkes that ben here,
Bodye and soule ben myne, · bothe gode and ille.
For Hym-self seyde, · that Sire is of Hevene, 480
Yif Adam ete the apple, · alle shulde deye,
And dwelle with us develes; · this thretynge He made;
And He that Sothenesse is · seyde thise wordes;
And sitthen I seised · sevene hundreth wyntre,
I leve that Lawe nil naughte · lete Hym the leest.' 485
    'That is sothe,' seyde Sathan, · 'but I me sore drede,
For thow gete hem with gyle · and his gardyne breke,
And in semblaunce of a serpent · sat on the appeltre,
And eggedest hem to ete · Eve by hir-selve,

            462: Lift up your gates [O ye princes], etc.

And toldest hir a tale, · of tresoun were the wordes;   490
And so thow haddest hem oute · and hider atte laste.
It is noughte graythely geten · there gyle is the rote.'
'For God wil nought be bigiled,' · quod Gobelyn, 'ne
    bi-japed;
We have no trewe title to hem, · for thorwgh tresoun were
    thei dampned.'
'Certes, I drede me,' quod the devel, · 'leste Treuth wil
    hem fecche.   495
  This thretty wynter, as I wene, · hath He gone and
    preched;
I have assailled Hym with synne, · and some tyme yasked
Where He were God or Goddes Sone. · He gaf me shorte
    answere.
And thus hath He trolled forth · this two and thretty
    wynter,
And whan I seighe it was so · slepyng, I went,   500
To warne Pilates wyf · what dones man was Jhesus;
For Juwes hateden hym · and han done hym to deth.
I wolde have lengthed His lyfe; · for I leved, yif he deyede,
That His soule wolde suffre · no synne in His syghte.
For the body, whil it on bones yede, · aboute was ever,   505
To save men fram synne · yif hem-self wolde.
And now I se where a soule · cometh hiderward seyllynge,
With glorie and with grete lighte — · God it is, I wote wel.
I rede we flee,' quod he, · 'faste alle hennes.
For us were better noughte be · than biden his syghte.   510
For thi lesynges, Lucifer, · loste is al owre praye.
Firste thorw the we fellen · fro Hevene so heighe;
For we leved thi lesynges · we loupen oute alle with the;
And now for thi last lesynge · ylore we have Adam,
And al owre lordeship, I leve, · a londe and a water;   515
    Nunc princeps huius mundi eicietur foras.'
  Efte the lighte bad unlouke, · and Lucifer answered,
'What lorde artow?' quod Lucifer, · *'quis est iste?'*

      515: Now the prince of this world will be cast out.
      517: Who is that?

'*Rex glorie*,' · the lighte sone seide,
'And lorde of myghte and of mayne, · and al manere vertues;
   dominus virtutum;
Dukes of this dym place, · anon undo this gates,   520
That Cryst may come in · the Kynges Sone of Hevene.'
And with that breth Helle brake · with Beliales barres;
For any wye or warde, · wide opene the gatis.

   Patriarkes and prophetes, · *populus in tenebris*,
Songen seynt Johanes songe, · *ecce agnus dei*.   525
Lucyfer loke ne myghte, · so lyghte hym ableynte.
And tho that Owre Lorde loved · in-to his lighte he laughte,
And seyde to Sathan, 'lo! here · my soule to amendes
For alle synneful soules · to save tho that ben worthy.
Myne thei be and of me, · I may the bette hem clayme.   530
Al-though resoun recorde, · and right of my-self,
That if thei ete the apple · alle shulde deye,
I bihyghte hem nought here · Helle for evere.
For the dede that thei dede · thi deceyte it made;
With gyle thow hem gete · agayne al resoun.   535
For in my paleys, Paradys, · in persone of an addre,
Falseliche thow fettest there · thynge that I loved.

   Thus ylyke a lusarde · with a lady visage,
Thevelich thow me robbedest; · the Olde Lawe graunteth,
That gylours be bigiled, · and that is gode resoun;   540
   Dentem pro dente, & oculum pro oculo.
Ergo, soule shal soule quyte, · & synne to synne wende,
And al that man hath mysdo · I, man, wyl amende.
Membre for membre · bi the Olde Lawe was amendes,
And lyf for lyf also, · and by that Lawe I clayme it,
Adam and al his issue · at my wille her-after.   545
And that deth in hem fordid, · my deth shal releve,
And bothe quykke and quyte · that queynte was thorw
   synne;
And that grace gyle destruye · good feith it asketh.

518: The King of Glory.   519: The Lord of Virtues.
524: the people in darkness.   525: behold, the Lamb of God.
540: a tooth for a tooth, and an eye for an eye.   541: Therefore.

So leve it noughte, Lucifer, · ageine the Lawe I fecche hem,
But bi right and by resoun · raunceoun here my lyges: 550
    Non veni soluere legem, sed adimplere.
Thow fettest myne in my place, · ageines al resoun,
Falseliche and felounelich; · gode faith me it taughte,
To recovre hem thorw raunceoun, · and bi no resoun elles,
So that with gyle thow gete · thorw grace it is ywone.
Thow, Lucyfer, in lyknesse · of a luther addere, 555
Getest by gyle · tho that God loved;
   And I, in lyknesse of a leode, · that Lorde am of Hevene,
Graciousliche thi gyle have quytte: · go gyle ageine gyle!
And as Adam and alle · thorw a tre deyden,
Adam and alle thorwe a tree · shal torne ageine to lyve; 560
And gyle is bigyled · and in his gyle fallen:
    Et cecidit in foueam quam fecit.
Now bygynneth thi gyle · ageyne the to tourne,
And my grace to growe · ay gretter and wyder.
The bitternesse that thow hast browe · brouke it thi-selven,
That art doctour of deth · drynke that thow madest! 565
   For I, that am Lorde of Lyf, · love is my drynke,
And for that drynke to-day · I deyde upon Erthe.
I faughte so, me threstes yet, · for mannes soule sake;
May no drynke me moiste · ne my thruste slake,
Tyl the vendage falle · in the Vale of Josephath, 570
That I drynke righte ripe must · *resureccio mortuorum*,
And thanne shal I come as a kynge, · crouned with angeles,
And han out of Helle · alle mennes soules.
   Fendes and fendekynes · bifor me shulle stande,
And be at my biddynge · where so evre me lyketh. 575
And to be merciable to man · thanne my kynde it asketh,
For we beth bretheren of blode, · but noughte in baptesme
    alle.
Ac alle that beth myne hole bretheren · in blode and in
    baptesme,

        550: I came not to destroy the Law, but to fulfil it.
        561: And he fell into the pit which he made.
        571: the resurrection of the dead.

Shal noughte be dampned to the deth · that is with-outen
    ende;
    Tibi soli peccaui, &c.
It is nought used in Erthe · to hangen a feloun   580
Ofter than ones · though he were a tretour.
And yif the kynge of that kyngedome · come in that tyme,
There the feloun thole sholde · deth or otherwyse,
Lawe wolde, he yeve hym lyf, · if he loked on hym.
    And I, that am Kynge of Kynges, · shal come suche a
        tyme,   585
There dome to the deth · dampneth al wikked;
And yif lawe wil I loke on hem · it lithe in my grace,
Whether thei deye or deye noughte · for that thei deden ille.
Be it any thinge aboughte · the boldenesse of her synnes,
I may do mercy thorw rightwisnesse · and alle my wordes
    trewe.   590
And though holiwrit wil that I be wroke · of hem that
    deden ille.
    Nullum malum inpunitum, &c.
Thei shul be clensed clereliche · and wasshen of her synnes
In my prisoun Purgatorie, · til parce it hote,
And my mercy shal be shewed · to manye of my bretheren.
For blode may suffre blode · both hungry and akale,   595
Ac blode may nought se blode · blede, but hym rewe.' —
    Audiui archana verba, que non licet homini
      loqui. —
'Ac my rightwisnesse and right · shal reulen al Helle,
And mercy al mankynde · bifor me in Hevene.
For I were an unkynde Kynge · but I my kynde holpe,
And namelich at such a nede · ther nedes helpe bihoveth; 600
    Non intres in iudicium cum seruo tuo, domine.
Thus bi lawe,' quod Owre Lorde, · 'lede I wil fro hennes
Tho that me loved · and leved in my comynge.

    579: Against Thee only have I sinned, etc.
    591: No evil shall be unpunished.
    596: I heard the private words which it is not right for man to speak.
    600: Enter not, O Lord, into judgement with thy servant.

And for thi lesynge, Lucifer, · that thow lowe til Eve,
Thow shalt abye it bitter' — · and bonde hym with cheynes.
Astaroth and al the route · hidden hem in hernes,   605
They dorste noughte loke on Owre Lorde · the boldest of
    hem alle,
But leten hym lede forth what hym lyked · and lete what hym
    liste.
    Many hundreth of angeles · harpeden and songen,
        Culpat caro, purgat caro; regnat deus dei caro.
    Thanne piped Pees · of poysye a note,
'*Clarior est solito post maxima nebula phebus,*   610
Post inimicitias clarior est et amor.
After sharpe shoures,' quod Pees, · 'most shene is the sonne;
Is no weder warmer · than after watery cloudes.
Ne no love levere · ne lever frendes,
Than after werre and wo, · whan love and pees be
    maistres.   615
Was nevere werre in this worlde, · ne wykkednesse so kene,
That ne love, and hym luste, · to laughynge ne broughte,
And Pees thorw pacience · alle perilles stopped.'
'Trewes,' quod Treuth, · 'thow tellest us soth, bi Jhesus!
Clippe we in covenaunt, · and uch of us cusse other.'   620
'And lete no peple,' quod Pees, · 'perceyve that we chydde,
For inpossible is no thyng · to Hym that is almyghty.'
    'Thow seist soth,' seyde Ryghtwisnesse, · and rever-
    entlich hir kyste,
'Pees and pees here! · *per secula seculorum.*'
      Misericordia & veritas obuiauerunt sibi, iusticia
        & pax osculate sunt.
Treuth tromped tho, and songe · *te deum laudamus;*   625

608: The flesh sins, the flesh redeems from sin, the flesh reigns as
God of God.
610: After thick clouds the sun is brighter than usual, and love too
is brighter after a quarrel.
624: for ever and ever
    Mercy and truth met together,
    justice and peace kissed.
625: we praise Thee, O God.

And thanne luted Love · in a loude note,
  Ecce quam bonum, & quam iocundum, &c.
  Tyl the daye dawed · this damaiseles daunced,
That men rongen to the resurexioun; · and right with that I
    waked,
And called Kitte my wyf · and Kalote my doughter —
'Ariseth and reverenceth · Goddes resurrexioun,   630
And crepeth to the crosse on knees, · and kisseth it for a
    juwel!
For Goddes blissed body · it bar for owre bote,
And if afereth the fende, · for such is the myghte,
May no grysly gost · glyde there it shadweth!'

        626: Behold, how good, and how joyful, etc.

SECTION IV

The Vision of Antichrist

Passus XX

SECTION IV

The Vision of Antichrist

To Hell, allegiance! vows, to the blackest devil!
Conscience and Grace, to the profoundest pit!
William Shakespeare, *Hamlet*

Whan Nede had undernome me thus, · anon I felle aslepe,
And mette ful merveillously · that, in mannes forme,
Antecryst cam thanne, · and al the croppe of Treuthe
Torned it up so doune · and overtilte the rote,
And made Fals sprynge and sprede · and spede mennes
    nedes;   5
In eche a contre there he cam · he cutte awey Treuthe,
And gert Gyle growe there · as he a god were.
Freres folwed that fende, · for he yaf hem copes,
And religiouse reverenced hym · and rongen here belles,
And al the covent forth cam · to welcome that tyraunt,   10
And alle hise, as wel as hym, · save onlich folis;
Which folis were wel lever · to deye than to lyve
Lenger, sith Leute · was so rebuked,
And a fals fende Antecriste · over alle folke regned;
And that were mylde men and holy · that no myschief
    dredden,   15
Defyed al falsenesse · and folke that it used,
And what kynge that hem conforted · knowynge hem any
    while,
They cursed, and her conseille, · were it clerke or lewed.
   Antecriste hadde thus sone · hundredes at his banere,
And Pryde it bare · boldely aboute,   20
With a lorde that lyveth · after lykynge of body,
That cam agein Conscience · that kepere was and gyoure
Over kynde Crystene · and cardynale vertues.

G   77

'I conseille,' quod Conscience tho, · 'cometh with me, ye
  foles,
Into Unyte Holy-cherche · and holde we us there,   25
And crye we to Kynde · that he come and defende us,
Foles, fro this fendes lymes, · for Piers love the plowman.
And crye we to alle the comune · that thei come to Unite,
And there abide and bikere · agein Beliales children.'
  Kynd Conscience tho herde · and cam out of the
    planetes,   30
And sent forth his forejoures, · fevres and fluxes,
Coughes, and cardiacles, · crampes, and tothaches,
Rewmes, and radegoundes, · and roynouse scalles,
Byles, and bocches, · and brennyng agues;
Frenesyes, and foule yveles, · forageres of Kynde,   35
Hadde yprykked and prayed · polles of peple
That largelich a legioun · lese her lyf sone.
  There was — 'harrow and help! · here cometh Kynde,
With Deth that is dredful · to undone us alle!'
  The lorde that lyved after lust · tho alowde cryde   40
After Conforte, a knyghte, · to come and bere his banere.
'Al-arme! alarme!' quod that lorde, · 'eche lyf kepe his
  owne.'
  And thanne mette this men · ar mynstralles myghte pipe,
And ar heraudes of armes · hadden descreved lordes.
  Elde the hore · he was in the vauntwarde,   45
And bare the banere bifor Deth, · by righte he it claymed.
Kynde come after · with many kene sores,
As pokkes and pestilences · and moche poeple shente;
So Kynde thorw corupciouns · kulled ful manye.
  Deth cam dryvende after · and al to doust passhed   50
Kynges and knyghtes, · kayseres and popes;
Lered ne lewed, · he let no man stonde,
That he hitte evene · that evere stired after.
Many a lovely lady · and lemmanes of knyghtes
Swouned and swelted · for sorwe of Dethes dyntes.   55
  Conscience of his curteisye · to Kynde he bisoughte,
To cesse and suffre · and see where thei wolde

Leve Pryde pryvely · and be parfite Cristene.
  And Kynde cessed tho · to se the peple amende.
Fortune gan flateren thenne · tho fewe that were alyve,   60
And byhight hem longe lyf · and Lecherye he sent,
Amonges al manere men, · wedded and unwedded,
And gadered a gret hoste · al agayne Conscience.
  This Lecherye leyde on · with a laughyng chiere,
And with pryve speche · and peynted wordes,   65
And armed hym in ydelnesse · and in hiegh berynge.
He bare a bowe in his hande, · and manye blody arwes
Weren fethered with faire biheste · and many a false truthe.
With his untydy tales · he tened ful ofte
Conscience and his compaignye, · of Holicherche the
    techeres.   70
  Thanne cam Coveityse · and caste how he myghte
Overcome Conscience · and cardynal vertues,
And armed hym in Avaryce · and hungriliche lyved.
His wepne was al wiles · to wynnen and to hyden;
With glosynges and with gabbynges · he gyled the peple.   75
Symonye hym sente · to assaille Conscience,
And preched to the peple · and prelates thei hem maden,
To holden with Antecryste · her temperaltes to save

And come to the kynges conseille · as a kene baroun,
And kneled to Conscience in courte afor hem alle,   80
And gart Gode Feith flee · and Fals to abide,
And boldeliche bar adown · with many a brighte noble
Moche of the witte and wisdome · of Westmynster Halle.
He jugged til a justice · and justed in his ere,
And overtilte al his treuthe · with 'take this up
    amendement.'   85
And to the Arches in haste · he yede anone after,
And torned Civile in-to Symonye · and sitthe he toke the
    official;
For a mantel of menyvere · he made lele matrimonye
Departen ar deth cam, · and devors shupte.
   'Allas!' quod Conscience, and cried tho, · 'wolde Criste,
    of his grace,   90
That Coveityse were Cristene · that is so kene a fighter,
And bolde and bidyng · while his bagge lasteth.'
   And thanne lowgh Lyf, · and leet dagge his clothes,
And armed hym in haste · in harlotes wordes,
And helde Holynesse a jape · and Hendenesse a wastour,   95
And lete Leute and cherle · and Lyer a fre man;
Conscience and conseille · he counted it a folye.
   Thus relyed Lyf · for a litel fortune,
And pryked forth with Pryde · preyseth he no vertue,
Ne careth noughte how Kynde slow · and shal come atte
    laste,   100
And culle alle erthely creatures · save Conscience one.
Lyf leep asyde · and laughte hym a lemman,
'Heel and I,' quod he, · 'and hieghnesse of herte
Shal do the noughte drede, · noyther Deth ne Elde,
And to foryete sorwe · and yive noughte of synne.'   105
   This lyked Lyf · and his lemman Fortune,
And geten in her glorie · a gadelyng atte laste,
One that moche wo wroughte, · Sleuthe was his name.
Sleuthe wex wonder yerne · and sone was of age,
And wedded one Wanhope, · a wenche of the stuwes.   110
Her syre was a sysour · that never swore treuthe,

One Thomme Two-tonge · ateynte at uch a queste.

    This Sleuthe was war of werre · and a slynge made,
And threwe drede of dyspayre · a dozein myle aboute.
For care Conscience tho · cryed upon Elde,   115
And bad hym fonde to fyghte · and afere Wanhope.

    And Elde hent good hope · and hastilich he shifte hym,
And wayved awey Wanhope · and with Lyf he fyghteth,
And Lyf fleigh for fere · to Fysyke after helpe,
And bisoughte hym of socoure · and of his salve hadde, 120
And gaf hym golde, good woon · that gladded his herte,
And thei gyven hym agayne · a glasen houve.
Lyf leved that lechecrafte · lette shulde Elde,
And dryven awey Deth · with dyas and dragges.

    And Elde auntred hym on Lyf · and atte laste he hitte 125
A Fisicien with a forred hood, · that he fel in a palsye,
And there deyed that doctour · are thre dayes after.
'Now I see,' seyde Lyf, · 'that surgerye ne Fisyke
May noughte a myte availle · to medle agein Elde.'
And in hope of his hele · gode herte he hente,   130
And rode so to Revel, · a ryche place and a merye,
The Companye of Conforte · men cleped it sumtyme.
And Elde anone after me · and over myne heed yede,
And made me balled bifore · and bare on the croune,
So harde he yede over myn hed · it wil be seen evre. 135
    'Sire evel-ytaughte Elde,' quod I, · 'unhende go with the!
Sith whanne was the way · over mennes hedes?
Haddestow be hende,' quod I, · 'thow woldest have asked
    leve!'
    'Ye! leve lordeyne,' quod he, · and leyde on me with age,
And hitte me under the ere, · unethe may ich here; 140
He buffeted me aboute the mouthe · and bette out my
    tethe,
And gyved me in goutes, · I may noughte go at large.
And of the wo that I was in · my wyf had reuthe,
And wisshed ful witterly · that I were in Hevene.
For the lyme that she loved me fore · and leef was to fele, 145
On nyghtes namely · whan we naked were,

I ne myght in no manere · maken it at hir wille,
So Elde and she sothly · hadden it forbeten.

And as I seet in this sorwe · I say how Kynde passed,
And Deth drowgh niegh me, · for drede gan I quake,   150
And cried to Kynde · out of care me brynge.
'Loo! Elde the hoore · hath me biseye,
Awreke me, if yowre wille be, · for I wolde ben hennes.'

'Yif thow wilt ben ywroken, · wende in-to Unite,
And holde the there evre · tyl I sende for the,   155
And loke thow conne somme crafte · ar thow come thennes.'
'Conseille me, Kynde,' quod I, · 'what crafte is best to lerne?'

'Lerne to love,' quod Kynde, · 'and leve of alle othre.'
'How shal I come to catel so · to clothe me and to fede?'
'And thow love lelly,' quod he, · 'lakke shal the nevre   160
Mete ne worldly wede, · whil thi lyf lasteth.'

And there, by conseille of Kynde, · I comsed to rowme
Thorw contricioun and confessioun, · tyl I cam to Unite;
And there was Conscience constable · Cristene to save,
And biseged sothly · with sevene grete gyaunts,   165
That with Antecrist helden · hard agein Conscience.

Sleuth with his slynge · an hard saut he made,
Proude prestes come with hym, · moo than a thousand,
In paltokes and pyked shoes · and pisseres longe knyves,
Comen agein Conscience; · with Coveityse thei helden.   170
'By Marie,' quod a mansed preste · of the marche of
        Yrlonde,
'I counte namore Conscience, · bi so I cacche sylver,
Than I do to drynke · a draughte of good ale!'
And so seide sexty · of the same contreye,
And shoten agein with shotte · many a shef of othes,   175
And brode hoked arwes · 'Goddes herte', and 'His nayles',
And hadden almost Unyte · and holynesse adowne.

Conscience cryed, 'Helpe, · clergye, or ellis I falle
Thorw inparfit prestes · and prelates of Holicherche.'
Freres herden hym crye · and comen hym to helpe,   180
Ac, for thei couth noughte wel her craft, · Conscience
        forsoke hem.

Nede neghed tho nere · and Conscience he tolde
That thei come for coveityse · to have cure of soules —
'And for thei arn poure, par aventure · for patrimoigne hem
  failleth,
Thei wil flatre, to fare wel, · folke that ben riche;   185
And sithen thei chosen chele · and cheytif poverte,
Lat hem chewe as thei chese · and charge hem with no cure!
For lomer he lyeth · that lyflode mote begge,
Than he that laboureth for lyflode · and leneth it beggeres.
And sithen freres forsoke · the felicite of Erthe,   190
Lat hem be as beggeres · or lyve by angeles fode!'
 Conscience of this conseille tho · comsed forto laughe,
And curteislich conforted hem · and called in all freres,
And seide, 'Sires, sothly · welcome be ye alle
To Unite and Holicherche, · ac on thyng I yow preye, 195
Holdeth yow in Unyte · and haveth none envye
To lered ne to lewed · but lyveth after yowre rewle.
And I wil be yowre borghe, · ye shal have bred and clothes,
And other necessaries inowe · yow shal no thyng faille,
With that ye leve logyk · and lerneth for to lovye.   200
For love laft thei lordship, · bothe londe and scole,
Frere Fraunceys and Dominyk · for love to ben holy.
 And if ye coveyteth cure, · Kynde wil yow teche,
That in mesure God made · alle manere thynges,
And sette hem at a certeyne · and at a syker noumbre, 205
And nempned names newe · and noumbred the sterres;
  *Qui numerat multitudinem stellarum, & omnibus
   eis nomina vocat, &c.*
Kynges and knyghtes · that kepen and defenden,
Han officers under hem, · and uch of hem certeyne;
And if thei wage men to werre · thei write hem in noumbre,
Or wil no tresorere hem paye, · travaille thei nevre so
  sore.   210
Alle other in bataille · ben yholde bribours,
Pilours and pykehernois · in eche a place ycursed.

206: Who numbers the host of stars, and to them all He gives names,
etc.

Monkes and monyals · and alle men of religioun
Her ordre and her reule wil · to han a certeyne noumbre.
Of lewed and of lered · the lawe wol and axeth   215
A certeyn for a certeyne · save onelich of freres.
For-thi,' quod Conscience, 'by Cryst, · Kynde Witte me
    telleth,
It is wikked to wage yow, · ye wexeth out of noumbre!
Hevene hath evene noumbre, · and Helle is with-out
    noumbre;
For-thi I wolde witterly · that ye were in the Registre,   220
And yowre noumbre undre notaries sygne · and noyther
    mo ne lasse!'
    Envye herd this · and heet freres to go to scole,
And lerne logyk and lawe · and eke contemplacioun,
And preche men of Plato · and preve it by Seneca,
That alle thinges under Hevene · oughte to ben in
    comune.   225
    And yit he lyeth, as I leve, · that to the lewed so precheth,
For God made to men a lawe · and Moyses it taughte,
        Non concupisces rem proximi tui
And evele is this yholde · in parisches of Engelonde,
For persones and parishprestes · that shulde the peple
    shryve,
Ben curatoures called · to knowe and to hele,   230
Alle that ben her parisshiens · penaunce to enjoigne,
And shulden be ashamed in her shrifte; · ac shame maketh
    hem wende,
And fleen to the freres · as fals folke to Westmynstre,
That borweth and bereth it thider · and thanne biddeth
    frendes
Yerne of foryifnesse · or lenger yeres lone;   235
    Ac whil he is in Westmynstre · he wil be bifore,
And make hym merye · with other mennes goodis.
And so it fareth with moche folke · that to the freres
    shryveth,
As sysours and excecutours · thei wil yyve the freres
    227: Do not covet the thing which belongs to your neighbour.

A parcel to preye for hem · and make hem-self myrye   240
With the residue and the remenaunt · that other men
     biswonke,
And suffre the ded in dette · to the day of dome.
   Envye herfore · hated Conscience,
And freres to philosofye · he fonde hem to scole,
The while Coveytise and unkyndenesse · Conscience
     assailled.   245
In Unite Holycherche · Conscience helde hym,
And made Pees porter · to pynne the gates
Of alle taletellers · and tyterers in ydel.
Ypocrisye and he · an hard saut thei made.
Ypocrisye atte gate · hard gan fighte,   250
And wounded wel wykkedly · many a wise techer,
That with Conscience acorded · and cardinale vertues.
Conscience called a leche · that coude wel shryve,
'Go salve tho that syke ben · and thorw synne ywounded.'
Shrifte shope sharpe salve · and made men do penaunce   255
For her mysdedes · that thei wroughte hadden,
And that Piers were payed · *redde quod debes*.
   Somme lyked noughte this leche · and lettres thei sent,
Yif any surgien were in the sege · that softer couth plastre.
Sire Lief-to-lyve-in-leccherye · lay there and groned;   260
For fastyng of a Fryday · he ferde as he wolde deye.
'Ther is a surgiene in this sege · that softe can handle,
And more of phisyke bi fer · and fairer he plastreth,
One Frere Flaterere · is phisiciene and surgiene,'
Quod Contricioun to Conscience. · 'Do hym come to
     Unyte,   265
For here is many a man · herte thorw Ypocrisie.'
   'We han no nede,' quod Conscience, · 'I wote no better
     leche
Than persoun or parissh prest · penytancere or bisshop,
Save Piers the plowman · that hath powere over hem alle,
And indulgence may do · but if dette lette it.   270
I may wel suffre,' seyde Conscience, · 'syn ye desiren,

         257: give back what you owe.

That Frere Flaterer be fette · and phisike yow syke.'
   The Frere her-of herde · and hyed faste
To a lorde for a lettre · leve to have to curen,
As a curatour he were · and cam with his lettres   275
Baldly to the bisshop · and his brief hadde,
In contrees there he come in · confessiouns to here,
And came there Conscience was · and knokked atte gate.
   Pees unpynned it · was porter of Unyte,
And in haste asked, · 'what his wille were?'   280
'In faith,' quod this frere, · 'for profit and for helthe
Carpe I wolde with Contricioun, · and therfore come I
    hider.'
   'He is sike,' seide Pees, · 'and so ar many other,
Ypocrisie hath herte hem · ful harde is if thei keure.'
'I am a surgien,' seide the segge, · 'and salves can make;   285
Conscience knoweth me wel · and what I can do bothe.'
'I preye the,' quod Pees tho, · 'ar thow passe ferther,
What hattestow, I preye the? · Hele noughte thi name.'
   'Certes,' seyde his felow, · 'Sire Penetrans-domos.'
'Ye, go thi gate,' quod Pees, · 'by God, for al thi phisyk,   290
But thow conne somme crafte · thow comest nought her-
    inne!
I knewe such one ones, · noughte eighte wynter passed,
        289: Sir Enterer-of-Houses.

Come in thus ycoped · at a courte there I dwelt,
And was my lordes leche · and my ladyes bothe.
And at the last this limitour, · tho my lorde was out,   295
He salved so owre wommen · til somme were with childe!'
Hende-speche het Pees · opene the gates —
'Late in the frere and his felawe · and make hem faire chere.
He may se and here · so it may bifalle,
That Lyf thorw his lore · shal leve Coveityse,   300
And be adradde of deth · and with-drawe hym fram pryde,
And acorde with Conscience · and kisse her either other.'
Thus thorw Hende-speche · entred the frere,
And cam in-to Conscience · and curteisly hym grette,
'Thow art welcome,' quod Conscience, · 'canstow hele the
     syke?   305
Here is Contricioun,' quod Conscience, · 'my cosyn,
     ywounded,
Conforte hym,' quod Conscience, · 'and take kepe to his
     sores;
The plastres of the persoun · and poudres biten to sore,
He lat hem ligge overlonge · and loth is to chaunge hem;
Fro Lenten to Lenten · he lat his plastres bite.'   310
     'That is overlonge,' quod this limitour, · 'I leve I shal
        amende it.' —
And goth and gropeth Contricioun · and gaf hym a plastre
Of 'a pryve payement · and I shal praye for yow,
For alle that ye ben holde to · al my lyf tyme,
And make yow, my lady, · in masse and in matynes,   315
As freres of owre fraternite, · for a litel sylver.'
     Thus he goth and gadereth · and gloseth there he
        shryveth,
Tyl Contricioun hadde clene foryeten · to crye and to wepe,
And wake for his wykked werkes, · as he was wont to done.
For confort of his confessour, · Contricioun he lafte,   320
That is the sovereynest salve · for alkyn synnes.
     Sleuth seigh that · and so did Pryde,
And come with a kene wille · Conscience to assaille.
Conscience cryde eft · and bad Clergye help hym,

And also Contricioun · forto kepe the yate.   325
'He lith and dremeth,' seyde Pees, · 'and so do many other;
The Frere with his phisik · this folke hath enchaunted,
And plastred hem so esyly · thei drede no synne.'
    'Bi Cryste,' quod Conscience tho, · 'I wil bicome a
        pilgryme,
And walken as wyde · as al the worlde lasteth,   330
To seke Piers the plowman · that Pryde may destruye,
And that freres hadde a fyndyng · that for nede flateren,
And contrepleteth me, Conscience; · now Kynde me avenge,
And sende me happe and hele · til I have Piers the
        plowman!'
And sitthe he gradde after grace · til I gan awake.   335

EXPLICIT HIC DIALOGUS PETRI PLOWMAN.

        336: Here ends the discourse of Piers the ploughman.

APPENDIX A

Some Critical Opinions of
PIERS PLOWMAN

R. W. CHAMBERS, *Man's Unconquerable Mind*

We should think of Langland as the poet of Catholicism, certainly; but we may also think of him in the way Shelley does in the *Defence of Poetry*, as throwing a bridge over the stream of time, and uniting the modern and ancient world. We may sometimes get more out of marking how the poets unite the ages, than by separating them into compartments: 'Dante the poet of Catholicism, Shakespeare of Feudalism. . . .'

The spiritual successors of *Piers Plowman* are to be found among the Puritans and the rebels, with Fox and Bunyan and Whitfield and Blake. I would go further and say that we find in *Piers Plowman* the determination to follow the search for 'Saint Truth' wherever it may lead, which has marked some later searchers who, in the words of Canon Streeter, 'have cheerfully for truth's sake renounced, not merely the good things of this life, but the hope of a life to come.' But no renunciation such as Canon Streeter had in mind can be found in *Piers Plowman*. . . . The hope (and the fear) of the life to come is there everywhere present. . . .

Piers Plowman combines things [in the political and religious life of England] which have since been separated, and so, in its broad appeal, is the most thoroughly English of all our religious poems; any Englishman who will take trouble to understand it can sympathize with it. *Piers Plowman* stands to win as the spirit of unity wins, for that is one of its great messages:

Cry we to all the commons that they come into Unite,
And there abide and do battle against Belial's children.

NEVILL COGHILL

The article *The Character of Piers Plowman Considered from the B Text*[1] deals with a subject which is for the most part out of the range of the reader of a selective edition — the general structural unity of the poem. It is, however, one of the most important contributions to the study of the poem and a knowledge of its contents may well be of use and interest to the reader of any part or parts of the poem.

Professor Coghill shows by detailed analysis of the work that Langland was no sprawling, undisciplined artist, but that on the contrary the poem was carefully planned so as to explain the three lives, Dowell, Dobet and Dobest. The virtues of each life are illustrated and given concrete embodiment in the person of Piers. Thus Piers is not so much a character with personal idiosyncrasies (though Langland is artist enough to give him individual credibility) as a living emblem of a way of life. One cannot do better unless one has first done well, or do best unless one has first done better: thus the virtues inherent in Piers who exemplifies Dowell recur (with additions) in Dobet, and again appear with yet further additions in Dobest. Mr. Coghill shows how, at each new appearance, Piers has acquired new moral qualities exactly fitting to the abstract virtues necessary to the way of life that is being described — whether the life-active of laymen, the life-contemplative of priests, or the life-authoritarian of bishops. Thus, it is perfectly logical that Piers should appear at one time as a labourer, at another as a king, or Christ, or Adam. If a king lives truly the life of Dowell he *lives* the Piers we see in Dowell; if Christ takes on human nature and lives truly the life of Dobet, then He *lives* the Piers of Dobet — but it is Christ, not Piers, who harrows Hell, for Piers is at all times the *human* embodiment of a way of life, and only in Christ's earthly ministry did He elect to

iuste in Piers armes,
In his helme and in his haberioun · *humana natura.*

I reproduce below some passages of Mr. Coghill's article which bear immediate relationship to the sections of the poem included in this edition.

[1] Published in *Medium Aevum,* vol. 2 (1933), and written by Nevill Coghill.

'Into this [allegorical] structure, at certain premeditated points, irrupts the figure of Piers Plowman. Perhaps in no other work of equal scope does the hero appear so seldom in person; but every appearance in this poem has calculated significance.

'Piers first "put forth his hed" when the secular world of Action had confessed its sins and was attempting satisfaction for them (the third part of a valid penance) by seeking St. Truth. This would seem a late entry for the hero; but if he be accepted as an emblem of Dowel, of the Active Unlettered Life as it should be, there is no earlier point at which he could have made his appearance; for a glance at the analysis of the first section [discussed earlier in Professor Coghill's article] shows that the first three sub-sections are quite general, and deal with all the world, not omitting the Governing Class, and as such are not amenable to the simple solution of Dowel, but ask the higher wisdom of Holy Church who offers advanced reflections on the purposes of human life under the hand of God; her teaching is quite beyond the province of Piers as Dowel, just as is the advice later given to the King. Up to this point, therefore, there is no mention of either Dowel or Piers. The Confession of the Seven Sins is again quite general; and it is prompted by the sermon of Reason who proves that the pestilences were in consequence of sin and for no other reason. Here again it would not have been becoming to the trend of the allegory for simple unlettered Dowel to usurp the position and authority of Reason in preaching repentance to the world. And therefore the figure of Piers is still withheld. Indeed he remains hidden until the more exalted and theoretic advice has failed. In their efforts to seek the Shrine of Truth the worldlings "blustreden forth as bestes", not knowing which way to turn. They had had *spiritual* advice from their Confessor, and were trying to follow it; what they lacked was *practical* advice; and this, as might be expected, the finical Palmer, all decked out and arrayed with the trophies of his pilgrimages, could not supply. For practical advice a practical man is needed and therefore, modestly, but with the assurance of one who speaks from fifty years' experience, Piers emerges as a leader, "the type of ideal honest man", in short Dowel.

'At first he offers them spiritual advice in practical form, a sort of map of the common road to Truth (i.e. Honesty,

Evenhandedness), a Mosaic *Carte du Tendre*; and in this there is nothing which the ordinary unlettered Christian was not supposed to know . . . the Ten Commandments, the obligations of Penance and Amendment and Charity, et cetera. But even this is too abstruse for the for-wandered world:

"This were a wicked way · but who-so had a gyde"

So with a still more practical insight Piers sets them all to *work*. That had been his own solution to the problem of seeking Truth; that had been his own life:

"I dyke and I delue · I do that Treuthe hoteth."

That, in fact, was as much as, in his simplicity, he knew, or needed to know, in the Active Life of Dowel. . . .'

*   *   *   *   *

'Allegory, once believed to be the life of poetry, is now commonly thought to be the death of it; this may have come about from the general changes in English ways of thinking; but I suggest that it comes more particularly from the contempt in which the allegorical aspects of later works such as *The Faerie Queene* are commonly held. Hazlitt has voiced this contempt once and for all; the difference between the allegory of Spenser and the allegory of Langland is the difference between a pleasing formal artifice and a natural growth; there is a topiary effect in *The Faerie Queene*; the allegory is the carpentered work of an unmatched artist-craftsman; but in *Piers Plowman* the allegory is organic, the bone in the body. His allegory we now have to understand by an intellectual process not unlike deliberate translation, for we are unaccustomed to reading in allegory. Just as the reader of a French book is not *reading French* as long as he mentally translates it into his own tongue while reading, so in Langland we are not reading allegory as long as we are analysing and making an argued interpretation. The real reader of a foreign tongue thinks immediately in that tongue; the language of allegory asks the same unselfconscious comprehension.'

J. J. JUSSERAND, *Piers Plowman*

We owe to Chaucer's horror of vain abstractions the picturesque individuality of each one of his personages; all classes of society are represented in his works; but the types which impersonate them are so clearly characterized, their singleness is so marked, that, on seeing them, we think of them alone and of no one else; individuals occupy all the foreground, and the background of the canvas disappears; we are so absorbed in the contemplation of this or that man, that we think no more of the class, the ensemble, the nation.

The active and actual passions of the multitude, the subterranean lavas which simmer beneath a brittle crust of good order and regular administration, all the latent possibilities of volcanoes which this inward fire represents, are, on the contrary, always present to the mind of our visionary. Rumblings are heard and herald the earthquake. The vehement and passionate England that produced the great revolt of 1381 and the heresy of Wyclif, that later on will give birth to Cavaliers and Puritans, is contained in the essence in Langland's work; we divine, we foresee her. Chaucer's book is, undoubtedly, not in contradiction to that England, but it screens and allows her to be forgotten.

Multitudes, like men, have their individuality. It seems as if Chaucer had, in depicting his characters, expended all his gifts of individualising. His horror of abstractions does not extend to multitudes; his multitudes are abstract ones. Excepting two or three profound observations, such as a man of his genius could not fail to make, he shows us the mass of humanity changeable, uncertain, 'unsad, untrue'; remarks applicable to the crowds of all times and recorded in the works of all authors.

From that point of view, Langland is very different from his illustrious contemporary. He excels in the difficult art of conveying the impression of a multitude, motionless, painted on the back scene of his stage and fit to serve for any play; his crowds of human beings have a character and temper of their own; he does not stop long to describe them; still, we see them; when they are absent from the stage, we hear them; in the distance we feel their approach. They are not any crowd, they are an English crowd. . . .

. . . in the dim recesses where he casts the rays of his lantern, Langland spares none; his ferocious laugh is reverberated by the walls, and the scared night-birds take flight. His mirth is not the mirth of Chaucer, itself less light than the mirth of France; not the joyous peal of laughter which rang out on the Canterbury road, welcoming the discourses of the exhibitor of relics, and the

far from disinterested sermons of the friar to sick Thomas; it is a
woeful and terrible laugh, harbinger of the final catastrophe and
judgement. What they have heard in the plain of Malvern, the
accused ones will hear again in the valley of Jehoshaphat.

They have now no choice, but must come out of their holes;
and they come forward into the light of day, hideous and
grotesque, saturated with the moisture of their dismal vaults; the
sun blinds them, the fresh air makes them giddy. They present a
sorry figure. Unlike the pilgrims of Canterbury, they derive no
benefit from the feelings of indulgence that softens our hearts on
a gay April morning. They will learn to know the difference
between the laugh that pardons and the laugh that kills. Langland takes them up, lets them fall, and takes them up again; he
never wearies of this cruel sport. . . .

C. S. LEWIS, *The Allegory of Love*

The greatest English allegory of this period falls a little outside
our subject. I relinquish *Piers Plowman* with the less regret because I leave it in better hands than mine;[1] my only anxiety is
lest, by passing it over, I may seem to place it in a false isolation
from the literature of the period, and thus to confirm certain
misunderstandings. Scholars more interested in social history
than in poetry have sometimes made this poem appear much less
ordinary than it really is as regards its kind, and much less extra-
ordinary as regards the genius of the poet. In fact, its only oddity
is its excellence; in *Piers Plowman* we see an exceptional poet
adorning a species of poetry which is hardly exceptional at all.
He is writing a moral poem, such as Gower's *Miroir de L'Homme*
or Gower's Prologue to the *Confessio Amantis*, and throwing in,
as any other medieval poet might have done, a good deal of satire
on various 'estates'. His satire falls heaviest where we should
expect it to fall — on idle beggars, hypocritical churchmen, and
oppressors. Like Chaucer he reverences knighthood. Even as a
moralist he has no unique or novel 'message' to deliver. As a cure
for all our ills he can offer us only the old story — do-well, do-bet
and do-best. His advice is as ancient, as 'conventional', if you
will, as that of Socrates; not to mention names more august. It is
doubtful whether any moralist of unquestioned greatness has
ever attempted more (or less) than the defence of the universally

[1] N. K. Coghill, *Medium Aevum*, vol. 2, no. 2.

acknowledged; for 'men more frequently require to be reminded than informed'. As a politician, Langland has nothing to propose except that all estates should do their duty. It is unnecessary, I presume, to state that his poem is not revolutionary, nor even democratic. It is not even 'popular' in any obvious sense. A poem every way unsuitable for recitation cannot have been addressed to those who could not read; and any one who supposes that Langland had in view an audience very different from the audience of Gower and Chaucer may be advised to imagine the probable results of reading aloud in a tavern or on a village green such lines as the following:

> The whiles I quykke the corps, quod he, called am I *Anima;*
> And whan I wilne and wolde, *Animus* ich hatte;
> And for that I can and knowe, called am I *Mens;*
> And whan I make mone to God, *Memoria* is my name.

Or, if he prefers,

> Thus is relacion rect ryht as adiective and substantif
> Accordeth in alle kyndes with his antecedent.

Langland is a learned poet. He writes for clerks and for clerkly-minded gentlemen. The forty-five manuscripts, and the presence of quotation from Langland in Usk's *Testament of Love,* prove that he did not write in vain. It would have been strange if he had. He offered to his educated contemporaries fare of a kind which they well understood. His excellent satiric comedy, as displayed in the behaviour of the seven Deadly Sins, belongs to a tradition as old as the *Ancren Riwle;* and his allegorical form and pious content were equally familiar.

What is truly exceptional about Langland is the kind, and the degree, of his poetic imagination. His comedy, however good, is not what is most characteristic about him. Sublimity — so rare in Gower, and rarer still in Chaucer — is frequent in *Piers Plowman.* The Harrowing of Hell, so often and so justly praised, is but one instance. There is not much medieval poetry that does not look pale if we set it beside such lines as these:

> Kinde huyrde tho Conscience, and cam out of the planetes
> And sente forth his foreyours, fevers and fluxes —
> Ther was 'Harrow!' and 'Help! Here cometh kynde,
> With Deth that is dredful to undo us alle!'

The Lord that lyuede after lust, tho aloude criede
After Comfort, a knyght, to come and bere hus baner.
'Alarme, alarme! quath that Lord, 'eche lyf kepe hus
    owene!' . . .[1]

[Professor Lewis goes on to mention Langland's ability to render
'imaginable what before was only intelligible' in which, on
occasions he surpasses even Dante. . . .]

Doubtless such heights are rare in Langland, as they are rare
in poetry at all; but the man who attains them is a very great
poet. He is not, indeed, the greatest poet of his century. He
lacks the variety of Chaucer, and Chaucer's fine sense of language: he is confused and monotonous, and hardly makes his
poetry into a poem. But he can do some things which Chaucer
cannot, and he can rival Chaucer in Chaucer's special excellence of pathos.

G. R. Owst

Professor Owst's *Literature and Pulpit in Medieval England* is
one of the most important background studies for readers of
medieval religious writings. One particular passage, however, in
which he reaffirms a statement made in his earlier *Preaching in
Medieval England* has since been regarded by many critics as an
unwarrantable overstatement. Shortly before his death, Professor Owst revised *Literature and Pulpit* (Blackwell, 1961) and
considerably modified his earlier view. Below are reproduced the
original statement and the recent modification.

'In his last sketch of English Medieval Literature, the late
Professor W. P. Ker put forward what apparently he considered
to be an important argument for single authorship of the *Vision
of Piers Plowman* and its three well-known versions. Of "the
tone of thought in the poem", he remarks —

It is hard to believe that there were two authors in the same
reign who had the same strong and weak points, the same in-
consistencies, wavering between lively imagination and formal
allegory, the same indignation and the same tolerance. *Piers
Plowman* is one of the most impartial of all reformers. He

[1] C-Text reading.

makes heavy charges against many ranks and orders of men, but he always remembers the good that is to be said for them. His remedy for the evils of the world would be to bring the different estates — knights, clergy, labourers and all — to understand their proper duty. His political ideal is the commonwealth as it exists, only with each part working as it was meant to do; the king making the peace, with the knights to help him, the clergy studying and praying, the commons working honestly, and the higher estates also giving work and getting wages.[1]

'Now, in the course of our study of Sermon Satire and Complaint against the ruling class we had occasion to note, strangely enough, another and kindred suggestion of uncommon impartiality of view in social matters attributed to John Wycliffe by Professor G. M. Trevelyan.[2] That view, it will be recalled, proved, when we examined it in the light of the sermons, to be false in its limited application to the Reformer, but thoroughly true and typical if applied to medieval homilists *as a whole*. The present case is precisely analogous. So far from being in any way unique, this "tone of thought" in *Piers Plowman* appears, on investigation, to be in perfect accord with that of the most commonplace orthodox preaching of the times, indeed a perfect echo in every respect of the Church's message to the world. If in his final phrase here Professor Ker means nothing more than "getting wages" in the figurative sense of the Gospel Parable of the Husbandmen, we may accept his summary forthwith as an accurate statement of Langland's constructive social gospel, and proceed at once to hear what our preachers have to say upon the subject. The task should make a fitting conclusion to our studies not only of the sermons, but also of the great poem itself. For, we have already been led to discover in the former the sources of its "formal allegories", its "lively imagination" along with many of its characters, and more recently still of its "indignation" and its "heavy charges against many ranks and orders of men". With the due establishment of this one further point of indebtedness, the present writer's original thesis may claim to be well nigh proven — namely, that the *Vision of Piers Plowman* "represents nothing more nor less than the quintessence of English medieval preach-

[1] *English Literature Medieval* (Home University Library), p. 200.
[2] *England in the Age of Wycliffe* (London, 1899), p. 202.

ing gathered up into a single metrical piece of unusual charm and vivacity" "[1] (Cambridge edition).

The revised edition continues as far as ' "heavy charges against many ranks and orders of men" ' (and then has) 'delivered with an impressive "impartiality". Varieties of interpretation still continue to pour forth unabated and many problems remain. But, with the due establishment of this further point of indebtedness, we may surely claim that the medieval pulpit helped to fashion much of the poet's fundamental thinking.'[2]

[1] *Preaching in Medieval England*, p. 295.
[2] Professor Owst kindly drew my attention to this revision.

APPENDIX B

Works to which reference has been made and Select Bibliography

WORKS TO WHICH SPECIFIC REFERENCE HAS BEEN MADE
IN THIS EDITION

M. D. Anderson, *Drama and Imagery in English Medieval Churches* (Cambridge University Press, 1963)

M. W. Bloomfield, *The Seven Deadly Sins: An Introduction to the History of a Religious Concept, with Special Reference to Medieval English Literature* (Michigan State College Press, 1952)

E. H. Phelps Brown and S. V. Hopkins, *Economica*, New Series, vol. xxii (The London School of Economics and Political Science, 1955)

E. K. Chambers, *The Medieval Stage* (Oxford University Press, 1903)

E. K. Chambers, *English Literature at the Close of the Middle Ages: Oxford History of English Literature*, vol. 2, pt. 2 (Oxford University Press, reprinted 1948)

R. W. Chambers, *Man's Unconquerable Mind* (Jonathan Cape, 1939)

N. K. Coghill, 'The Character of Piers Plowman Considered from the B Text' (*Medium Aevum*, vol. 2, Basil Blackwell & Mott, 1933)

N. K. Coghill, *Visions from Piers Plowman*, a modernization in alliterative verse (Phoenix House, 1949)

H. Craig, *English Religious Drama of the Middle Ages* (Oxford University Press, 1955)

J. F. Davis (ed.), revised E. Olszewska, *Langland, Piers Plowman, Prologue and Passus I–VII Text B* (University Tutorial Press)

E. T. Donaldson, *Piers Plowman, the C-Text and Its Poet* (Yale University Press, 1949)

100   SELECTIONS FROM PIERS PLOWMAN

T. S. Eliot, *Collected Poems 1909–1935* (Faber & Faber, 1936)

T. S. Eliot, 'Andrew Marvell', contained in *Selected Essays* (Faber & Faber, revised edition 1951, p. 293)

A. Fortescue, *The Holy Week Book* (Burns, Oates & Washbourne, 1913)

J. F. Goodridge, *Piers the Plowman*, translated into modern English (Penguin, 1959)

W. W. Greg (ed.), *The Chester Play of Antichrist* (Oxford University Press, 1935)

W. H. Hulme, *The Middle English Harrowing of Hell and Gospel of Nicodemus, Now First Printed from All the Known MSS.* (Early English Text Society, Extra Series 100, London, 1907)

J. J. Jusserand, *Piers Plowman* (T. Fisher Unwin, 1894)

J. N. D. Kelly, *Early Christian Creeds* (Longmans, Green & Co., 1950)

D. Knowles, *The Religious Orders in England* (Cambridge University Press, 1955)

C. S. Lewis, *The Allegory of Love, A Study in Medieval Tradition* (Oxford University Press, reprinted 1951)

J. M. Manly, J. J. Jusserand and R. W. Chambers, *The Piers Plowman Controversy* (Early English Text Society, Original Series, Extra Volume 139 B, Kegan Paul, Trench & Co. and Oxford University Press, 1910)

J. R. H. Moorman, *Church Life in England in the 13th Century* (Cambridge University Press, 1945)

A. Nicoll, *World Drama* (Harrap, 1957)

G. R. Owst, *Preaching in Medieval England* (Cambridge University Press, 1926)

G. R. Owst, *Literature and Pulpit in Medieval England* (revised edition, Blackwell, 1961; original edition, Cambridge University Press, 1933)

A. W. Pollard, *English Miracle Plays, Moralities and Interludes* (Oxford University Press, 1890; reprinted 1954)

E. Power, *Medieval English Nunneries* (Cambridge University Press, 1922)

E. Power, *Medieval People* (Penguin, 1954; 10th edition, Methuen, 1963)

M. Rose, *The Wakefield Mystery Plays* (John Evans, 1961)

E. Salter, *Piers Plowman, An Introduction* (Basil Blackwell & Mott, 1962)

W. W. Skeat, *Langland's Vision of Piers Plowman, Text B*

(published for the Early English Text Society by the Oxford University Press, reprinted 1950)

W. W. Skeat, *The Vision of William Concerning Piers the Plowman, together with Vita de Dowel, Dobet et Dobest and Richard the Redeles*, 4 vols. (published for the Early English Text Society by N. Trübner & Co., 1885)

The Register of John le Romeyn, Archbishop of York, 1286–1296 (The York Registers, published for the Surtees Society by Andrews & Co., Durham, and B. Quaritch, London, 1917)

SELECT BIBLIOGRAPHY

In addition to the works listed above, the following may be of interest:

M. W. Bloomfield, *Piers Plowman as a Fourteenth-century Apocalypse* (Rutgers University Press, New Brunswick, New Jersey, 1961)

A. H. Bright, *New Light on Piers Plowman* (Oxford University Press, 1928)

N. Coghill, *Langland — Piers Plowman* ('Writers and their Work' series, Longmans, Green & Co., 1964)

M. R. James (trans.), *The Apocryphal New Testament* (Oxford University Press, 1953)

J. J. Jusserand, *English Wayfaring Life in the Middle Ages* (T. Fisher Unwin, 1892)

G. Kane (ed.), *Piers Plowman—the A-version: Will's Visions of Piers Plowman and Do-well* (Athlone Press, 1960). Complete edition in preparation.

G. Kane, *Piers Plowman: the Evidence for Authorship* (Athlone Press, 1965)

J. Lawlor, *Piers Plowman, An Essay in Criticism* (Edward Arnold, 1962)

W. W. Skeat, *The Vision of William Concerning Piers the Plowman, in Three Parallel Texts* (Oxford University Press, 1886; reprinted 1954), 2 vols.

D. Traversi, 'Langland's *Piers Plowman*', essay in *The Age of Chaucer* (Penguin, 1954)

I have not mentioned works which refer exclusively to the A- or C-Texts.

Critical Notes

SECTION I

The May morning setting was conventional in medieval allegorical poetry — particularly love poetry where the link of Spring and youthfulness is a functional part of the tradition. Conventional, too, was 'dream-allegory' in which the poet — or 'the Dreamer', who becomes a character in his own right — falls asleep and dreams allegorically. (For detailed discussion, *vide* C. S. Lewis, *The Allegory of Love, passim.*) Elizabeth Salter, *Piers Plowman: An Introduction*, pp. 58 *et seq.*, points out that the dreaming of the poet is constantly shown to be allowed by the grace of God: it is no ordinary dreaming but a vision of the ultimate realities of life. The dreaming is 'in its context, no escapist wish, but an eager desire to return to the source of life'.

l. 3. Dr. Whitaker, in his 1813 edition, paraphrases, 'not like an anchorite who keeps his cell, but like one of those unholy hermits who wander about the world to hear and see wonders.' Skeat comments, 'It may simply . . . express the author's opinion of hermits in general.'

l. 11. Langland's debt to sermon-literature is inestimable, and nowhere is this more clearly seen than in the *form* of this poem. Langland, like the homilists, sees the world as a field; Heaven as a tower; Hell as a dungeon.

Often the soul of man was imagined as a castle besieged by the Wicked One. Owst writes (*Literature and Pulpit in Medieval England*, p. 77), 'From one of the two texts most freely quoted [from the Vulgate] — Intravit Jesus in castellum — there springs at an early date the idea of the Blessed Virgin as a Castle, into which the Saviour entered at His Incarnation, a feudal stronghold protecting Him from the Devil in an otherwise defenceless world.'

The Castle, too, sometimes represented the Castle of Evil, held by the Seven Deadly Sins. This arises from the Palm Sunday text '*Ite in castellum quod contra vos est*'. Here, by interpretation, Christ commands the preacher to go and loose the ass, that is the evil man 'bound in the Devil's chains'. [Owst]

The image appears also in medieval drama,[1] whose influence may be seen on *Macbeth* with the Castle with a 'Hell-gate Devil-porter', a 'devilish' and 'Hell-hound' king, a 'fiend-like' queen, and league with 'instruments of darkness'; and the Castle whose king is 'full of grace', and whence Malcolm, whose father was 'most sainted' and who leads 'God's soldiers', gathers his forces.

l. 39. *Qui turpiloquium, etc.* The reference is probably to Titus i, vv. 10–12. Skeat regards the passage as eliptical and incomplete; but the sense is clear if we adopt Dr. J. S. Davis's suggestion of recognizing that 'but' is implied: 'What St. Paul says of them I will not expound it here (but) he who speaks lewdly is Lucifer's servant.'

l. 44. **roberdes knaves:** Thieves who often used violence. (It has been suggested that the name derives from Robin Hood's followers.) Hence Robert the Robber, l. 469 of Section II.

l. 54. **Walsyngham:** A highly popular resort for pilgrims. The pilgrimage to Walsingham, in particular, aroused the anger of Wyclif's followers.

l. 56. **to ben knowen fram othere:** Cf. l. 527 of Section II of this edition for details of signs worn by pilgrims so that in their supposed holiness they should be 'distinguished from others'.

l. 58. The four orders of friars were: Carmelites, Augustines, Dominicans and Franciscans.

l. 62. Cf. the 'double-worsted' semi-cope of Chaucer's Friar (*General Prologue*, l. 262).

---

[1] *Vide* particularly *The Castell of Perseverance* (written *circa* 1405), where the castle stands 'with watyre abowte the place, if any dycke may be mad ther it schal be pleyed'. The Seven Deadly Sins appear, as does a priest called Confession, who leads Mankind to repentance, and also 'the iiij dowters schul be clad in mentelys, Mercy in wyth, rythwysnesse in red, Trewthe in sad grene, and Pes al in blake, and they schul pleye in the place al to gedyr tyl they brynge up the sowle'. There is a convenient summary of this earliest extant Morality play in the Introduction, pp. xlv *et seq.*, of A. W. Pollard's *English Miracle Plays*. The reader is recommended to read this if he wishes to understand the communality of medieval literary ideas, e.g. after Mankind's being safely lodged in the Castle of Perseverance by Confession and Shrift, he awaits the fresh attacks of his enemies — and, as Old Age weakens him, he is attacked by the Devil and the Seven Deadly Sins. (Cf. the Antichrist section of this edition.)

l. 65. Plagues, storms, etc., were often considered God's punishments for man's evil. Cf. Reason's sermon (Section II, ll. 13 *et seq.* in this edition) where the great storm of 15th January, 1362, and also the outbreaks of plague are said to derive 'obviously from downright pride'. (For more examples of misfortunes at this time being attributed to wickedness *vide* J. J. Jusserand, *Piers Plowman*, pp. 19–20.) More than a third of the population of England died of plague between 1348 and 1351, and many more were killed by it in later epidemics.

l. 68. Cf. the description of Chaucer's Pardoner, *G.P.*, ll. 669 *et seq.*, and Prologue and Epilogue to *The Pardoner's Tale* for remarkably similar pinpointing of the iniquitous system of pardon-selling by the Pope through rogues who were happy enough to cheat the superstitious and ignorant in order to gain money. Usually there was fierce rivalry between parish priests and pardoners (cf. priest *v.* friar preaching in Section II, l. 143, and the note in this edition). Sometimes, however, the priest and pardoner shared the profits.

l. 80. Skeat notes: 'We must consider it as slightly humorous, meaning — "But you may be sure that it is never against the bishop that he preaches." '

l. 86. 'To seken a chaunterie for soules' (*G.P.*, l. 510), i.e. gain an easy income by saying masses for the dead at St. Paul's. Both Langland and Chaucer deplore this, but cf. the life of Langland (Introduction p. xviii). E. T. Donaldson in *Piers Plowman, The C-Text and its Poet* puts forward the alternative explanation that, 'Langland's priests may have gone to London because it was the chief source of ecclesiastical and political preferment, where benefices were most readily bought and sold.'

l. 87. **bachelers:** Novices in the church and bachelors of arts. It was very common for men who had studied in the universities to take secular employment. Hence, the masters (of arts) and doctors (of divinity) in the same line. Chaucer considers it noteworthy that his Clerk of Oxford had *not* taken Holy Orders.

l. 92. i.e. the clergy look for lucrative, and often lay, employment.

ll. 93–4. 'Formerly, the three principal courts of law, the King's Bench, the Common Pleas, and the Exchequer had a separate jurisdiction. The Exchequer decided only such cases as related to the collection of the revenue, and hence the ecclesiastics who held office in it are said here to *challenge*, i.e. to *claim* the King's debts from the various *wards* or divisons of the city. The *wardmote* is the court, or *meeting*, held in each ward. They also claimed for the King all *waifs* and *strays*, i.e. property without an owner and strayed cattle' (Skeat).

l. 104. The Cardinal Virtues are Prudence, Temperance, Fortitude and Justice.

l. 129. **Serjaunts:** Serjeants at law — the King's legal servants selected from the most eminent barristers. *Vide* Chaucer's Serjeant at Law, *G.P.*, ll. 309 *et seq.*

l. 136. *-estre:* Often, but not invariably, denotes feminine gender.

l. 142. 'The false accusation of unchastity against a queen is an ancient story. . . . In 1338 the *joculator* Herbertus told it at St. Swithin's, Winchester, of Emma, the wife of Canute, and this version may have been known to Langland, who quotes a line *Dieu vous saue, Dame Emme*, which looks like a refrain.' (E. K. Chambers, *Oxford History of English Literature*, vol. ii, part 2, p. 155.)

l. 151. The simplicity of clothing of Holychurch contrasts with the splendour of false Lady Meed, who appears in the next passus. The reference is to Revelation xvii. 4 (the description of the Whore of Babylon); and xix. 8 (the description of the Church, Christ's Bride): 'And to her was granted that she should be arrayed in fine linen, clean and white: for the fine linen is the righteousness of saints.'

l. 163. **Five wittis.** Common Wit, imagination, fantasy, estimation and memory. But these were sometimes confused with the Five Senses, i.e. sight, speech, taste, touch and hearing.

l. 168. Cf. Ecclesiasticus xxix. 21 : 'The chief thing for life is water, and bread, and clothing, and an house to cover shame.'

l. 179. 'Though he blamed wine for that wicked deed.'

l. 200. Render unto Caesar, etc., Matthew xxii. 21.

l. 216. It is an old belief that the tree on which Judas hanged himself was an elder.

l. 233. **trewthe:** i.e. God, King of the Tower on the Eastern Hill, and truth, that part of man that is godly.

l. 239. Luke viii. 21 : 'My mother and my brethren are these

which hear the word of God, and do it.' So placed by Skeat;
but it is not certain to which passage Langland refers.

l. 248. 'Protect men and women who desire the whole truth.'

l. 249. 'Never leave them for love or money.'

SECTION II

The Dreamer wakes at the point where the King, nobles and
commons of England enter church for Matins. He tells his beads,
sleeps again and dreams of the service, which by now has pro-
gressed as far as the sermon. The preacher (Reason) exhorts all
estates in the congregation, the lords and the commons, to cease
to shirk the responsibility of disciplining those in their care,
and to work hard and without hypocrisy. We must all seek St.
Truth.

The preacher then stands aside for another priest, Repentance,
who conducts the Confessional Service. Thus the Field of Folk
turns towards the Tower of Truth and, led by Piers the labourer,
goes to seek the Tower. Allegorically, mankind repents of its sins
and seeks God through honest work. We are reminded of
Chaucer's Plowman who 'wolde thresshe and therto dyke and
delve For Christes sake'. Or again of George Herbert's 'A
servant with this clause Makes drudgery divine'.

l. 13. This passage is evidence of the date of composition of the
poem. Here, the outbreaks of the plagues of 1349 and 1362
are referred to (*vide* Skeat's *EETS* edition Text B, Preface
II, p. iv). See also note on Section I. l. 65. in the present
edition.

l. 24. A mid-fourteenth century alliterative poem, discussing the
social problems of the time, was called *Winner and Waster*.
It is probable that Langland knew the poem, and the juxtaposition of the two words in l. 25 seems more than coincidental.

l. 28. Crowley's Text (*vide* Introduction, p. xix) reads Stowne,
i.e. Stone.

l. 29. **wyven pyne**: Wives' punishment, i.e. (probably) the
ducking-stool.

l. 31. The fantastic and costly head-dresses of women were
frequently ridiculed by moralists (cf. Chaucer's Wife of
Bath, whose Sunday coverchiefs weighed ten pounds). A

silver half-mark was worth 6s. 8d., a groat was worth 4d. For some indication of the value of money in the second half of the fourteenth century, it may be noted that a labourer in the building trade earned 3d. a day; a craftsman in the same trade earned 5d. Wages were considerably lower before the Black Death, when labourers were plentiful (vide E. H. Phelps Brown and S. V. Hopkins, Economica, New Series, vol. xxii, pp. 195 et seq.).

l. 36. Notice how the 'power of pestilence' is a constant dread in the people's minds, and it is easy to understand how this might tempt them to over-indulge their children.

l. 38. 'The dearer the child, the more should one teach him.' A medieval proverb, as Reason suggests in the previous line. Cf. the proverb of Hendyng (circa 1300): 'Luef child lore byhoueth.'

l. 43. Hypocrisy among the clergy is emphasized also by Chaucer (G.P., ll. 478 et seq.) whose idealized Parson first wrought and afterwards taught.

l. 56. Matthew xxv. 12.

l. 57. Pilgrims to the shrines of saints such as St. James should rather seek St. Truth (i.e. God). Jusserand (Piers Plowman, p. 141) quotes from the C-Text, and writes: 'Will they ever know the real place where they might find St. James? Will they suspect that St. James should be sought "ther poure syke lyggen (sick people lie), in prisons and in poore cotes (cottages)"? . . . They seek St. James in Spain, and St. James is at their gates; they elbow him each day, and they recognise him not.'

l. 58. Treuthe: Here means God, the Holy Ghost.

l. 75. Lechery and Gluttony were often linked in this way in discussions of the Seven Deadly Sins. Cf. Wife of Bath's Prologue, l. 464, 'For after drinking (wine) on Venus moste I thynke.' Also, Pardoner's Tale, l. 481, '. . . the fyr of lecherye, That is annexed unto glotonye.'

l. 77. mea culpa: From the Confessional. ('Peccavi nimis cogitatione, locutione, et opere: mea culpa' — 'I have sinned excessively in thought, word and deed: mine is the blame.')

Initially, Envy is seen here as a friar. At this point it is convenient to note Langland's method of working. A development in sermons was to illustrate the Sins by lively little character sketches of the sin in action, and giving the *characters the profession most closely beset by the sin.* The older method was to let the sin consort with actual characters (exactly as Wrath does in this text). Langland vacillates between the two, and in Sloth he works with the newer method (*vide* Owst, *Literature and Pulpit*, pp. 87–90).

l. 87. *Vide* Owst, *Literature and Pulpit*, pp. 450 *et seq.*, for adder and dog illustrations in medieval sermons, and for parallels to Langland's Envy: 'This fals ypocrites and bacbytors, thei will com to the churche . . . but yet thei will bacbite here even-cristen [fellow-Christians].'

l. 93. A 'weye of Essex chese' would be about half a ton. The Essex 'weye' was unusually large.

l. 108. The bowl was probably of little value, and the sheet was torn, but Envy clings to this trash and hates those who now have it.

l. 122. Skeat explains: ' "Cannot any sugar or sweet thing (be found to) assuage my swelling, nor any expectorant drive it out of my heart, nor any kind of penance or shame (relieve me), except some one were (actually) to scrape my maw?" A forcible way of expressing the question — "can none but the most violent measures relieve my moral sickness?" *Diapenidion* answers almost exactly to the modern barley-sugar, being a kind of sweet stuff twisted into a thread, and used to relieve coughs, &c.'

l. 127. Envy takes 'sorry' in a different sense — he is *always* sorrowful (that others may have more than he has) (*vide* General Introduction, p. xiv, ll. 23 *et seq.*).

l. 130. 'Be' can mean 'be' or 'by'. Skeat translates, 'I caused detraction to be made by means of a broker to find fault with other men's ware.' Goodridge renders, 'I would use Backbite as my private agent. . . .'

l. 134. In this passage about friars, Langland pinpoints the major abuses that marked the Orders in the fourteenth century. St. Francis, seeing the growing worldliness of the monastic orders, had founded his Order of Brothers whose lives were to be truly Christlike. They should have no houses, they should work for their food and preach to the people. Only in times of necessity should alms be sought. St. Dominic, who at first favoured receiving of alms, later advised that provision for one day only was to be accepted. Spoiled by popularity, the later friars became increasingly

worldly, cf. the expensive friary implied by the friar who
offers to absolve Lady Meed (Passus III, l. 48):

'We han a wyndowe a wirchyng · wil   (a wirchyng =
   sitten us ful heigh;   being made)
Woldestow glase that gable · and grave
   there-inne thi name,
Siker sholde thi soule be · hevene to have.'   (siker = sure)

Sharp quarrels between friars and parish priests were frequent all over Europe, and centred on the three practices
involving prestige and profit of preaching, burying of the
dead and hearing confession.

l. 136. **I was sum tyme a frere:** Chaucer, too (*G.P.*, l. 257),
attributes wrath to his friar: 'And rage he koude, as it were
right a whelp.'

l. 138. The tree-image in discussion of the Seven Deadly Sins
was customary, cf. *Parson's Tale*: 'Of the roote of thise
sevene synnes, thanne, is Pride the general roote of alle
harmes. For of this roote spryngen certein braunches, as Ire,
Envye, Accidie or Slewthe, Avarice or Coveitise (to com-
mune understondynge), Glotonye, and Lecherye. And
everich of thise chief synnes hath his braunches and his
twigges, as shal be declared in hire chapitres folwynge.'

It is no accident that Langland and Chaucer direct their
satire against the greatest travesty of the intentions of the
founders of the Orders — the institution of limiters. In the
early years, *procurators* had been selected from the inmates
of the various houses to collect alms. These subsequently
developed into limiters — friars who paid a rent to their
houses to have exclusive begging rights in a particular area
or limit, and who expected to make a profit. Friar Huberd's
'purchas was wel bettre than his rente' (*G.P.*, l. 256).
Squalid disputes sometimes arose among various friaries as
to the extent of their begging territories.

    listres: *lectors* (or readers) were the lowest but one of
those who were in the Holy Orders of the Church. The
Orders ranged from *ostiary* (door-keeper) to bishop.

l. 142. St. Francis had stressed that the friars were to be sub-
servient to the parish priests: '*Si haberem tantam sapientiam
quantam Salamon habuit, et invenirem pauperculos sacerdotes
huius saeculi, in parochiis, in quibus morantur, nolo praedicare*

ultra voluntatem ipsorum.' For examples of friar *versus* priest sermons, *vide* Owst, *Preaching in Medieval England*, pp. 72 *et seq.*

l. 144. **possessioneres**: There had for a considerable time been argument between theologians concerning the rights and wrongs of mendicancy on the one hand, and church ownership of goods and property on the other. About 1370, the dispute flared into a practical politics between the friars (mendicants) and the 'possessioners' (the endowed religious — the older orders of monks and canons). A good deal of anti-clerical lay support, and also the support of Wyclif, was given to the friars. (For full discussion *vide* Dom David Knowles, *Religious Orders in England*, vol. 2, pp. 65 *et seq.*)

l. 149. **and by my spirualte libben**: The sins are in fact death to the spirit, and Langland uses this form of irony frequently. Cf. 'the grace of gyle', l. 207.

l. 150. **and riden aboute**: St. Francis had ruled that, far from travelling on horseback, the Friars Minor should walk barefoot.

l. 151. lit. 'I, Wrath, never rest so that I might not follow these wicked people', i.e., 'I, Wrath, never rest lest I might not pursue these wicked people. . . .'

l. 155. **I have be cook in hir kichyne**: From the end of the twelfth century monasteries and nunneries employed lay servants. St. Benedict's division of the day into learning, manual labour and divine service, had kept minds and bodies usefully occupied. When the first two were removed, the resulting tedium was an easy gateway for Wrath.

The abbess usually had separate rooms and her own servants, and — nuns being almost invariably recruited from aristocratic families — the temptation to live in their accustomed luxury was great. At the Dissolution, the Abbess of St. Mary's Winchester had her own house, cook, undercook, serving-woman, laundress and waiting gentlewoman. The larger houses often employed a male cook, and sometimes a gardener.

For lay-servants being the cause of Wrath, cf. the complaint at Heyning's in 1440: 'The prioress encourages the secular serving-women, whom she believes more than her sisters in their words, to scold the same her sisters' (*Lincoln-*

shire Visitations, ii, p. 133, quoted by Eileen Power, *Medieval English Nunneries*.)

l. 158. **Dame Johanne ... Dame Clarice:** The illegitimate daughters of the great were sometimes disposed of by being sent to convents.

l. 160. **a prestes file:** A stock medieval taunt. Even Wolsey himself sent an illegitimate child to a convent — and the practice was not uncommon among medieval clergy who had erred. But Langland's reference is more specific. It was sometimes required that papal dispensation should be given before an illegitimate prioress-elect could hold office. Dispensations *super defectu natalium* 'were common enough in the case of priests' (Power, *Medieval English Nunneries*). Wrath may, then, adduce two reasons for the disqualification of Dame Peronelle — her own illegitimacy, and the birth of her child. The case of Dame Peronelle's child is matched many times by contemporary medieval records.

Or it is possible that *file* means concubine. The *Nonna et Clericus* theme was frequent in fable and reality. (*Vide* Eileen Power, *Medieval English Nunneries, passim.*)

l. 163. **'thow lixte':** In a medieval sermon, the preacher remarks that Wrath is often a result of the work of Envy, and continues: 'Thus bygynneth stryf; and after these two cometh chidinge, with "Thou lixte" and "Thou lixt".' (MS Harl. 45, fols. 150–1, quoted by Owst in *Literature and Pulpit*.)

l. 166. **Seynte Gregorie:** 'It appears that some Abbesses did at one time attempt to hear the confessions of their Nuns ... but this practice, I apprehend, was soon stopped by Gregory ix, who has forbidden it in the strongest terms — Decretal. 1. v. tit. 38. C. x.' (Tyrwhitt's note on *Canterbury Tales* quoted by Skeat.)

l. 172. **And if I telle any tales, etc.:** *vide The Rule of St. Benedict*, chap. xxiii: 'If any brother shall be found ... a murmurer ... let him be admonished secretly by his superiors for a first and second time. If he do not amend, let him be publicly rebuked before all. But if even then he do not correct his life, let him suffer excommunication [i.e. exclusion from the table and oratory] ... if, however, he be perverse, let him undergo corporal punishment.'

l. 173. **to bred and to water:** St. Benedict forbade the eating of meat, except in cases of illness, and ordained that the allowance of wine should be withheld from those undergoing certain penances. The York registers, published by the Surtees Society, give detailed accounts of the punishing of private religious. E.g. *Register of John le Romeyn*, p. 132: 'Rogerus, videlicet, claustrum per annum non exeat; et ultimus sit in conventu, omnia quarta et sexta feria [Wednesdays and Fridays] per id tempus pane, cervisia, et leguminibus, ac in Quadragesima *omni sexta feria pane et aqua* sit contentus tantummodo.' [My italics.]

l. 189. **sire Hervy**: Skeat notes: 'Skelton has the same name for a covetous man. "And Harvy Hafter, that well coude picke a male." '

l. 198. **couthe have lopen the bettre**: could have been a better jumper (lit. could have leapt better).

l. 203. **a leef**: a leaf (of a book). The metaphor continues in **lessoun** (l. 204) and **donet** (l. 209).

l. 205. Wy, Weyhill near Andover, Hampshire, was famous for its fair. The fairs were the chief places for bulk-buying. There was also a fair at Winchester.

l. 207. Cf. Note on Section II, l. 127.

l. 209. **donet**: primer. From Aelius *Donatus* a fourth-century Latin Grammarian.

l. 210. 'In 1353, statutes were passed regulating the length and breadth of cloth' (Skeat).

l. 216. **She spak to spynnesteres**: The normal practice in the very important cloth-making industry was that the wool was passed from spinners and carders to the weavers, who in turn sold it to fullers, they to shearmen and finally the dyers bought the cloth. Sometimes the order was varied. Women and children would perform the spinning and carding operations in their cottages. (For a most interesting account *vide* Eileen Power, *Medieval People*, chapter on Thomas Paycock of Coggeshall.)

l. 220. Penny ale (thin ale) sold at 1*d.* a gallon, pudding-ale (rich ale) at 4*d.* Deceit of this kind was not confined to England, cf. the fifteenth-century German *Redentiner Osterspiel* in which Satan tries to repopulate Hell after the Harrowing. In a procession of sinners comes a barmaid: 'I was always able to make a lot of beer, Chiefly for this reason: I used an ample quantity of water. . . . Whenever I measured out beer for someone, I believe I never once forgot To serve

part from the second boiling; And thus I earned many a
penny.' (Quoted by Nicoll, *World Drama*, p. 155.)

l. 225. **'By cups at a time.'** 'She knew better than to measure it
in a gallon measure' (Skeat).

l. 231. The cross of Bromholm, in Norfolk, was traditionally
thought to have been made by Helena mother of Constan-
tine from the original cross. (*Vide* note on l. 54 of Section I.)

l. 239. The ability to speak French, hitherto a social asset, was,
in fact, losing its importance at this time. But Avarice
regards Norfolk — a remote, rural area — as having less
than the usual amount of French.

l. 242. Jews and Lombards, charging very high interest rates,
were the chief money lenders. Skeat notes: 'The Jews were
constantly accused of being the offenders whenever clipped
coin was found, which was very often. . . . It is clear enough
what Avarice did: he first clipped coins and then lent them,
taking a pledge which he hoped would not be redeemed.'
The coins were marked on the reverse with a cross. Cf.
Touchstone's pun (*As You Like It*, II, iv. 11): 'Yet I should
bear no cross, if I did bear you; for I think you have no
money in your purse.' Sacred Christian relics were accepted
by Jews as pledges for borrowed money.

l. 246. *miseretur & comodat:* Psalm cxi. 5 (Vulg.), Ps. cxii. 5
(A.V.).

l. 255. Avarice has, of course, charged such exorbitant interest
that the lords have been forced to sell their manors and
become merchants. Notice the slick humour with which
Avarice boasts of his cruelty.

l. 261. **as hende, etc.**: a proverb that appears in many languages,
sometimes in the form, 'While a dog gnaws a bone, he does
not desire company.'

l. 263. 'now may God never lend thee grace to make good use of
thy wealth in this world unless thou repent.'

l. 268. Cf. first note on Wrath, l. 134.

l. 274. *Seruus, etc.:* It is not known from what work the lines are
taken.

l. 279. Made good, i.e. repaid (as in Mod. Eng.).

l. 304. There are many homiletic parallels to the man who is on
his way to church and is enticed into an ale-house by his
greed. Cf. John Bromyard *Summa Praedicandi:* '*Volentes ire
ad verbum Dei (Diaboli) ducunt ad tabernam.*' And also, the

comparison between God's miracles in Church and the Devil's miracles in the tavern (in one the lame walk; in the other the fit become unable to stand, etc.) in Dan Michel's *Ayenbite of Inwite* (*circa* 1340). For full discussion *vide* Owst, *Literature and Pulpit*, pp. 425 *et seq*.

l. 312. **piones**: Seeds of the paeony. 'They were used as medicine, but sometimes also as a spice, as here' (Skeat). The day on which Glutton is tempted into the inn is a fasting-day — a Friday. From the residences of the inmates of the tavern, Skeat conjectures that Langland may have had in mind the Boar's Head in Eastcheap — made famous by Shakespeare's Sir Glutton, Sir John Falstaff.

l. 314. **and grete othes**: The swearing of the drunken man was a commonplace of sermon admonition, cf. the three drunkards in the *Pardoner's Tale* whose 'othes been so grete and so dampnable That it is grisly for to heere hem swere'. And also, l. 376 in this passage.

l. 319. Prostitutes were often compelled to live in Cock Lane, West Smithfield. Flemish women living in London were notorious for prostitution.

l. 321. **Sire Piers**: Sir was often used as a title of respect for a priest or monk.

l. 328. **new faire**: This is a reference to an old game called *handicapping* — a sort of mock-bartering. Hikke chooses Bette to be his deputy; Clement also chooses a deputy (whose name is not given); the two deputies estimate the comparative values of the hood and the cloak but are unable to arrive at a satisfactory conclusion. So Robyn is nominated an umpire. He decides that Hikke should have the cloak, Clement the hood. Clement, having been awarded the less valuable hood, is permitted to fill his cup at Hikke's expense. The punishment for disagreeing with the umpire is to buy a gallon of ale for Sir Glutton.

l. 348. **pater-noster**: For the irony of the whole passage *vide* General Introduction, p. xiv.

l. 353. **glewmannes bicche**: The performing dog of a minstrel.

l. 392. Accidia, in the early monastic examples of lists of the Seven Cardinal Sins, meant 'spiritual dryness'. In the Later Middle Ages it became transferred (as in the present passage) to idleness in the performance of religious duties — particularly in the case of clergy. Later still (e.g. in Marlowe's

Doctor Faustus), Sloth implied general laziness and was not specifically associated with religious duties. Langland's complaints against dissolute clergy are paralleled in the works of many fourteenth-century writers, e.g. Bromyard says that the chamberlain of the Sins in the Devil's Castle is Sloth, 'who draws the curtains and makes men lie for long in wantonness, and makes priests to celebrate after midday.' Elsewhere Bromyard complains of 'prelates and clergy who consume the goods of the Church . . . on prostitutes' while they 'celebrate (Mass) scarce once a year, or never at all'.

l. 402. This is the earliest literary reference to Robin Hood. Sir Edmund Chambers (*Oxford History Eng. Lit.*, vol. ii, part 2, p. 130) writes: 'It seems to me very likely that the story of the outlaw took its start from a Robin Hood . . . in 1354 . . . . If so, it was not long before, in Thucydidean phrase, he had won his way to the mythical. By about 1377 the Sloth of *Piers Plowman* claimed to know "rymes of Robyn Hood".'

Randolf: Either the Earl of Chester in King Stephen's reign, or his grandson who married Constance, widow of Geoffrey Plantagenet. He was earl from 1181 to 1232. Skeat favours the latter to explain this reference.

l. 413. **somer game:** 'It may be the same as *summerings* which Halliwell defines as: (1) Country rejoicings and wakes formerly in vogue on Midsummer Day; (2) riots and scolding matches (in the north of England). The fondness of the parson for loose stories suggests that the "cobblers" summer game "was more allied to ribald jesting than to athletic sports" ' (Davis).

l. 419. *Ite, missa est:* The concluding words of the Mass. 'When I come to the last words I've had enough.'

l. 424. Cf. William de Pagula, a vicar in the first half of the fourteenth century, who notes in his *Oculus Sacerdotis*: 'Priests . . . giving themselves up to sloth . . . ready to track the footprints of hares.' And also, the Monk, *G.P.*, whose whole desire was 'huntyng for the hare'.

l. 425. *Beatus vir:* Psalm i or cxi (Vulg.), cxii (A.V.); *Beati Omnes:* Psalm cxxvii (Vulg.), cxxviii (A.V.).

l. 427. **lovedayes:** Days for settlements of disputes by arbitration without taking the matter to court; the clergy took an active part in the proceedings. Cf. Chaucer's Friar, who could 'muchel help' on lovedays.

reves rekenynge: a reeve's accounts. The exact func-
tions of the reeves are not known — but they seem to have
performed much of the work that falls to the modern bailiff
on an estate. Chaucer's Reeve was accountable directly to
the lord of the estate.

l. 454. Beating the breast was regarded as a sign of humility.

l. 467. A famous cross once stood in Chester at a place now called
Roodee (i.e. Cross Island).

l. 469. **Robert**: See note to Section I, line 44; *Reddite:* i.e. restitution (Romans xiii. 7).

l. 473. **Dismas**: The name given to the repentant thief in the
Apocryphal Gospel of Nicodemus.

l. 474. *memento:* '*Remember* me, Lord, when thou comest into
thy kingdom' were the words spoken to Christ by the
repentant thief.

l. 475. 'Take pity on this thief, myself, who have not any money
with which to make restitution, and cannot hope to earn by
trade as much as I owe.'

l. 484. Luke xxiii. 39, '*Unus autem de his qui pendebant latroni-
bus.*'

l. 491. *O, felix, etc.:* From the Sarum Missal at the blessing of the
Paschal Candle on Holy Saturday: '*O certe necessarium Ade
peccatum et nostrum; quod Christi morte deletum est. O felix
culpa, que talem ac tantum meruit habere redemptorem.*' (O
truly necessary sin of Adam and of ourselves that Christ's
death blotted out; O happy fault that merited such a
redeemer.) Cf. the fifteenth century lyric 'Adam lay
i-bowndyn':

> Ne hadde the appil take ben,
> Ne hadde never our lady
> a ben hevene qwen.

(Had not the apple been taken, Our Lady would never have
been Queen of Heaven.)

l. 494. *Faciamus, etc.:* Genesis i. 26; *Et alibi* =and elsewhere, i.e.
in another text. The reference is to 1 John iv. 16.

Piers Plowman has often been adversely criticized for lack
of homogeneity. Often, however, a theme is sounded at an
important stage of the poem, and later developed. This
symphonic movement is well exemplified by comparing the
present passage with the third section of this edition. In par-

ticular, the Piers–Christ–Charity equation is seen in the text 'He that dwelleth in love dwelleth in God, and God in him'.

Elizabeth Salter, *Piers Plowman: An Introduction*, p. 48, discusses the long-argued problem of the artistic unity, or lack of unity, of the poem. She concludes that modern readers have searched in vain, or made special pleadings, for a type of unity which the poet never intended: 'The elusive "logic of the plan" of the poem can often be explained in the same terms as those appropriate to the literature of the medieval pulpit which in its anxiety to produce the fullest possible "drawing out" of its stated themes, allowed, even encouraged, the modifications of planned form by sudden departure from plan, and which maintained an over-all unity by a loose-knit, linking system of repetitions, corre-spondences and cross-references.'

Cf. also the passage:

> . . . for pylgrymes ar we alle;
> And in the apparaille of a pore man · and
>   pilgrymes lyknesse
> Many tyme god hath ben mette.'
>
>   (B. XI, 234–6)

l. 498. *Captiuam, etc.*: Eph. iv. 8.

l. 500. Noon is traditionally the hour of the Devil's greatest temptation of man. *Nones* covered the period from 12 noon to 3 p.m., and it was customary for monks to take their food at this time; the shedding of Christ's blood was spiritual food for the souls who had waited for the Light of Christ to free them from Satan's bondage in Hell.

l. 501. *Populus qui ambulabat, etc.*: Isaiah ix. 2. and cf. the introduction to section III, p. 50.

l. 506. *Non veni, etc.*: Matthew ix 13.

l. 508. A close verbal parallel to l. 225 of Section III. The anonymous author of the Old English *The Dream of the Rood* also depicts Christ as a 'young warrior'; in *Piers Plowman* the Warrior jousts in true medieval fashion, but Langland makes it clear that he intends us to recognize that the armour (or heraldic coat of arms) is Human Nature which Jesus wears for the battle with Death. *Verbum, etc.* John i. 14.

ll. 514, 515 and 516. *deus, tu, etc.*: Psalm lxxxiv. 7 (Vulg.), lxxxv.

6 (A.V.); *Beati, etc.:* Psalm xxxi, 1 (Vulg.); xxxii. 1 (A.V.); *Homines, etc.:* Psalm xxxv. 7 (Vulg.), xxxvi. 6 (A.V.).

l. 521. **blustreden forth as bestes:** Matthew ix. 36 *et seq.* 'But when he saw the multitudes, he was moved with compassion at them, because they fainted, and were scattered abroad, as sheep having no shepherd. Then said he unto his disciples, "The harvest truly is plenteous, but the labourers are few." ' This makes significant the symbol of Piers the labourer.

l. 526 (and cf. l. 542). Luke x. 4, 'Carry neither purse, nor scrip.' The pilgrims with the paraphernalia of badges and a begging-bowl were not such as Christ had desired.

l. 527. A pilgrim who had visited a shrine often wore a badge to signify that he had made the journey. Langland points out that those who make a practice of 'wandering by the way' (as Chaucer describes the journeys) and wearing the insignia of journeys of devotion, were not necessarily devout. This particular pilgrim has never heard of another looking for St. Truth (i.e. who sought God). Piers shows that honest work leads to St. Truth.

The self-confessed hypocrite on Chaucer's pilgrimage, the Pardoner, wore a 'vernycle sowed upon his cappe'. The signs mentioned in this passage are:

Canterbury: phials of holy oil (*ampulles*).
Galicia (shrine of St. James at Compostella): scallop shells.
Rome: keys.
Jerusalem: a palm — but later 'palmers' were not necessarily pilgrims who had visited Jerusalem. Also, a cross. The shrine of St. Veronica: it is said that St. Veronica wiped with her handkerchief the face of Jesus as He carried the cross. The handkerchief received an impression of His face. A 'vernicle' (diminutive of Veronica) was a copy of the handkerchief.

The convent of St. Catherine was at Sinai.
Cf. Section I, l. 56 and the note on that line. See also, Section II, l. 57.

l. 566. **for Seynt Thomas shryne:** i.e. for all the wealth in the shrine of St. Thomas à Becket. The shrine, made rich by pilgrims' offerings, was the wealthiest in England.

l. 575. Piers has just mentioned Abstinence, Humility, Charity, Chastity, Patience, Peace and Bounty. These were the con-

ventional antidotes for the Seven Deadly Sins, except that
Vigilance is here replaced by Peace — though there were
many variant lists. The remedies were known as the Seven
Virtues.

l. 578. **bi myne heved:** i.e. by my head! This was a common
medieval mild oath, cf. 'By my pan (=brain-pan)!'
Chaucer *Knight's Tale*, l. 1165.

l. 582. The wafer-seller means that there would be no point in
her trying to seek St. Truth as she is not related to the
Seven Virtues. Chaucer's Pardoner, in his sermon, mentions
these sellers of confectionery in a list of immoral types of
women.

l. 590. Notice the superstitious faith of the pardoner, who
imagines that he can win his way to Heaven without the
Seven Virtues, so long as he shows his pardons. Bishop's
letters were the seal of a bishop licensing the pardoner to
preach. Cf. *Prologue to the Pardoner's Tale*, l. 337: 'Oure lige
lordes (i.e. bishop's) seel on my patente, That shewe I first.'
Cf. also Section I, l. 69, in this edition.

l. 592. How dramatically accurate that the prostitute should
make her apparently customary lie — 'Say I'm your sister'
— to explain her being in a man's company. Mr. J. F.
Goodridge (Penguin translation, p. 118) closes the inverted
commas after 'sister', and the Dreamer comments, 'But
what became of these two I cannot tell.' This makes better
sense than the Skeat punctuation.

l. 595. **Perkyn** is a diminutive form of Peter.

For a general discussion of Piers' setting the Field of Folk
to work, see the excerpt from an article by Prof. Nevill
Coghill (Appendix A, p. 92).

SECTION III

l. 1. **I awaked:** He has been dreaming about the events of
Christ's life.

l. 6. **mydlenten Sondaye:** i.e. Mid-Lent Sunday, the Fourth
Sunday in Lent.

l. 14. i.e. 'What (coat of arms) does that man bear?'

l. 21. Cf. I Corinthians i. 30.

ll. 25 *et seq.* Mr. Goodridge tentatively suggests the following
translation of this difficult passage: 'Three things are

necessary for a lord who claims men's allegiance: the first is power, the second is a medium through which to show forth his power (and also that of his servant), and the third is that which he and his servant suffer.'

l. 42. For the story of Lazarus see Luke xvi. 19.

l. 63. **spye**: Because Hope looks out for the coming of the Messiah.

l. 68. The Law is sealed with the crucifixion and (because we there bear the sign of the cross) in baptism.

l. 72. 'Letters patent are writings, sealed with the Great Seal of England, whereby a man is enabled to do or enjoy that which otherwise of himself he could not. And they are so called, because they are *open*, ready to be shewed for confirmation of the authority thereby given.' Blount's *Law Dictionary*, quoted by Skeat; **roche**: i.e. the stone tablets on which the Law was given to Moses.

l. 83. *Vide* apocryphal books of Judith and Maccabees.

l. 90. **that** = those that; **sory** = are sorry.

l. 106. '. . . than to love and believe rogues as much as honest men.'

l. 110. It was customary in medieval homilies to depart from the account of the parable given by St. Luke as to the direction in which the man was travelling. In the Gospel he was travelling to Jericho, in Langland's story he was travelling towards Heaven (Jerusalem) when evil overcame him. Faith and Hope are incompetent to help him; Christ suffering for Mankind (i.e. Charity) alone has power of salvation from sin.

l. 117. Vulgate *Gospel according to S. Luke* has *semiuiuus*, i.e. half-alive.

l. 126. **Lyard**: A common name for a grey horse. Grey was a much admired colour for a horse.

l. 129. '(And he perceived) that he would never rise again.'

l. 133. *Lex Christi:* i.e. the Church and the New Testament.

l. 134. **newe market**: i.e. market-town.

l. 137. All pennies were silver in the Middle Ages.

l. 157. Plaisters were in common use, and there was a proverb, 'Patience is a plaister.'

l. 160. **wildernesse**: A common description in medieval allegory for the world in which mankind wanders seeking the right road. Cf. 'These three (i.e. the world, the flesh and the devil), like three robbers, fight against each believing man as long as we wander in the wilderness of this world.' *O.E. Homilies*, ed. Morris, quoted Skeat. Cf. also the early thirteenth century *Ancrene Wisse* (a devotional manual for a group of female recluses) in the section describing the Seven Deadly Sins: 'Thus my dear sisters in the wilderness in which you are travelling towards the people of God and Jerusalem — that is, the kingdom of Heaven — there are such beasts and serpents. . . . Of these seven beasts and of their offspring mention has already been made; they are those that, in the wilderness of solitary life, attempt to ruin all the travellers.'

l. 169. The idea that the Samaritan's horse denotes human flesh (*Caro* of mankynde) occurs in other religious works.

l. 204. To have wool (not linen) next to the body was an act of penance.

l. 208. 'Lolled about until Lent.'

l. 210. Till Palm Sunday. See the introduction to this section.

l. 211. *Gloria Laus:* opening words of the hymn sung by children on Palm Sunday.

l. 217. **galoches:** Skeat quotes evidence to support the view that these shoes were allowed only to knights or those of higher rank. **ycouped** = cut, i.e. probably decorated with patterns cut into the leather, as were the shoes of that young man in the height of fashion — Absolom in Chaucer's *Miller's Tale* — who had designs from St. Paul's Cathedral windows carved on his shoes.

l. 223. 'the fruit of Piers the Plowman': i.e. Mankind. This probably refers back to Passus XVI where the Tree of Charity is described. The fruits of the tree are good men, whom Satan steals and hoards in *limbo* — 'There is derkenesse and drede.'

l. 282. *Longeus* (i.e. *Longinus*): See introduction to this section, p. 46.

l. 309. **usurye:** All usury was considered evil.

ll. 316 *et seq.* The meeting of the four sisters was a popular episode in the Mystery plays (see note to l. 11 in Section I). Doubtless, memories of the plays determined much of Langland's detail in these descriptions. He was also probably influenced by Bishop Grosteste's *Chastel d'Amour*. (For detailed study of the influence see that work and Skeat's pinpointing of similarities.)

l. 343. 'What was lost by a tree, a tree shall redeem.' The reference is to the Tree of Knowledge in the Garden of Eden, and to the Cross. Probably inmixed with this idea is the legend of Seth's journey to Paradise. (See introduction to this section.)

l. 358. It was believed that a dead scorpion taken in drink was a remedy for a scorpion's sting.

l. 363. *Ars ut, etc.*: Occurs in the hymn 'Pange, lingua, gloriosi'.

l. 367. *He* in Middle English can represent Old English *heo* = *she*.

l. 382. *Ad vesperum, etc.*: Psalm xxix. 6 (Vulg.); xxx. 5 (A.V.).

l. 385. 'And granted to me, Peace, and to Mercy that we might be man's mainpreneurs. . . .' One who stood bail for another was called a *mainpreneur*.

l. 387. *In pace, etc.*: Psalm iv. 9 (Vulg.), iv. 8 (A.V.). For explanation of letters patent *vide* note on l. 72 of this section.

l. 440. A comet was thought to be accompanied by wonderful events — such as a change of kings.

l. 451. Simeon is mentioned in Luke ii. 25. For explanation of this reference see introduction to this section, p. 50.

l. 453. *gygas:* This appears to be a faulty reading. C-Text has 'Jesus as a giant'.

l. 462. *Attollite, etc.*: See introduction to this section.

l. 467. **Lazar:** See introduction to this section in the passage quoted from the *Gospel of Nicodemus*, p. 50.

l. 479. The good are imprisoned in *limbo*, the evil in Hell.

l. 486. Satan and Lucifer are here (as in the *Gospel of Nicodemus*) regarded as two different devils.

l. 512. **fellen fro hevene**: A reference to the story of the Fall of the Angels, in which Lucifer, stirred by pride, corrupts a number of the angelic host and wars against God and the Good Angels. As a punishment they are committed to Hell. The lie referred to here is explained in Passus I, ll. 111 *et seq.*, where it states that Lucifer fell from the fellowship of Heaven in a fiend's likeness,

> Into a deep dark hell · to dwell there for ever;
> And more thousands with him · than one could number,
> Leaped out with Lucifer · in loathsome form,
> For they believed in him · who had lied in this manner:
> *Ponam pedem in aquilone, et similis ero altissimo.*

(Modernized)   (Cf. Isaiah xiv. 13-14)

l. 523. Cf. also 464. As in the *Wakefield Mystery Harrowing of Hell*, the entry of Christ into Hell is spoken of in terms of a medieval siege. (A convenient edition, modernized in spelling, and including notes on the staging of the scenes, is *The Wakefield Mystery Plays*, ed. by Martial Rose.)

l. 538. **lusarde with a lady visage**: There are a number of examples in medieval art, both literary and visual, in which the serpent in the Garden is represented as a lizard with a woman's face, or as a snake with a woman's face. This was to emphasize the nature of evil: attractive in appearance and wicked at heart.

l. 539. **The Olde Lawe**: i.e. the Old Testament.

l. 550. *Non veni, etc.*: Matthew v. 17.

l. 561. *Et cecidit, etc.*: Psalm vii. 16 (Vulg.), vii. 15 (A.V.).

l. 570. It was thought (by extension of the suggestion in Joel iii) that the resurrection of mankind would be in the Valley of Jehoshaphat.

l. 579. *Tibi soli, etc.*: Psalm l. 6 (Vulg.), li. 4 (A.V.).

ll. 580 *et seq.* It was the practice to pardon a man who survived hanging — particularly if the king were present. Skeat quotes the case of Walter Wynkeburn in 1363, and suggests that Langland may well have been thinking of this very example: 'Walter Wynkeburn having been hanged at Leicester, after having been taken down from the gallows as a dead man, was being carried to the cemetery to be buried, but began to revive in the cart. To this man King Edward [III] granted pardon. . . .'

l. 591. *Nullum malum, etc.*: Pope Innocent, *De Contemptu Mundi*, lib. iii, cap. 15: *Ipse est iudex iustus . . . qui nullum malum praetexerit impunitum, nullum bonum irremuneratum.*

l. 593. 'Till the word "Spare thou" command it,' i.e. till *parce* be the signal word for their release.

l. 595. i.e., 'A man may perhaps allow his relations to be hungry and cold; but he won't see a relation bleeding without feeling compassion.'

    Audiui archana, etc.: 2 Cor. xii. 4.

l. 600. *Non intres, etc.*: Psalm cxlii. 2 (Vulg.), cxliii. 2 (A.V.).

l. 605. Astaroth is the eastern equivalent to Greek Aphrodite, and appears in many Mystery plays as a devil.

l. 608. *Culpat, etc.*: Occurs in hymn *Aeterne rex altissime* in Office of the Ascension in the Roman Breviary.

l. 610. Perhaps *nubila* was intended for *nebula*.

l. 617. 'That Love could not bring to laughter if He chose.'

ll. 623–624. The reading of the C-Text is slightly different and
gives the excellent sense — 'Thou sayest truth, said Righteousness, and reverently kissed Peace — and Peace kissed
her for ever and ever.' If we accept the reading of the
B-Text, we must read something like, 'Peace, and again I
say Peace be here, for ever and ever.'

l. 624. *Misericordia, etc.*: Psalm lxxxiv. 11 (Vulg.), lxxxv. 10 (A.V.).

l. 626. *Ecce quam, etc.*: Psalm cxxxii. 1 (Vulg.), cxxxiii. 1 (A.V.).

l. 631. **crepeth to the crosse on knees**: This was an established
act of penance.

SECTION IV

l. 1. The Poet has wandered 'sick at heart, I knew not where to
eat'. But Need shows him that the spirits of Temperance
and Poverty are close to God, who had said: 'The foxes
have holes, and the birds of the air have nests; but the Son
of Man hath not where to lay his head.'

l. 3. The Antichrist story was popular in medieval Europe, and
appears in poetry and drama. Politically, too, the situation
of Christ and Anti-Christ was suggested to the minds of the
people by the existence of the Great Schism — the dividing
of the Western Church in 1378 by the election of a rival
Pope at Avignon. The split remained until 1417. Biblical
authority for the Antichrist story is found in 1 John ii. 18–22,
2 John vii, 2 Thessalonians ii. 3 ('The Man of Sin') and in
The Revelation of St. John the Divine *passim* ('The Beast').

There is a good deal of doubt concerning the origin of the
legend which is found in developed form in the Middle
Ages. It is generally agreed that the amplified form of the
story is derived from the *Libellus de Antichristi* written in the
mid-tenth century by Abbot Adso of Toul. (*Vide* the pre-
fatory note on the Antichrist legend in *The Chester Play of
Antichrist*, ed. by W. W. Greg.) It is possible that, as
2 Thessalonians ii was read at Mass on Saturday in the
fourth week of Advent, an Office (or Service) play developed
from the text, and that the legend owes its origin to this
dramatic representation. (*Vide* H. Craig, *English Religious
Drama of the Middle Ages*, pp. 74 *et seq.*)

ll. 4–7. As might be expected, honest agricultural work — Pier's half-acre — advocated in the poem both in a literal and spiritual sense is quite contrary to Antichrist's destructive reign of disorder. Cf. note on l. 521 of Section II.

l. 9. Ironically, the last ringing of bells in the poem had been for the risen Christ (l. 628 of Section III).

l. 11. **folis**: Langland uses the word ironically. He is quoting from the worldly-wise followers of Antichrist who regard Christians as fools. Later (l. 24) Conscience uses the word bitterly.

l. 15. i.e. the 'fools' did not care greatly about the loss of goods or life. If a king were to befriend them for a while, the followers of Antichrist would curse the king and those who had advised the 'fools'.

l. 20. Pride, because it is the chief of the Deadly Sins in most lists (*vide* Bloomfield *The Seven Deadly Sins*, p. 105). In *The Castell of Perseverance*, Pride bears the Devil's banner as he leads in the Seven Deadly Sins against Mankind. (Cf. note on l. 11 of Section I.)

l. 30. Nature 'came out of the planets' because it was thought that the planets influenced men's health. Chaucer's Doctor of Medicine was 'grounded in astronomye' (*G.P.*, l. 414).

l. 80. Covetousness kneels before Conscience to make a show of holiness.

l. 83. Westminster Hall, the location of the royal courts of law.

l. 85. 'Take this upon amendment', i.e. 'Here is some money, now surely we can alter the matter to something more agreeable.'

l. 86. **the Arches,** a nickname for the Archbishop of Canterbury's consistory courts in the church of St. Mary de Arcubus (St. Mary-le-Bow). The name derives, of course, from the structure of the church.

l. 87. '. . . and reduced the Law to Simony — not forgetting to bribe the chancellor of the diocese' (J. F. Goodridge's translation).

l. 89. The marriage service had 'Till death us depart'.

l. 93. A popular (and often satirized) custom of the day was to cut the edges of clothes into slits, or 'dags'.

l. 122. **a glasen houve**: i.e. 'a glass hood', an item of clothing that was only apparently protective. The expression was proverbial.

l. 136. The Dreamer — who here merges with the poet — makes

. K

a last bid for self-respect. But Old Age destroys every refuge of false personal dignity. The Dreamer is left toothless, crippled and impotent. At that point, he is reminded that only one thing gives man personal worthiness — 'Learn to love, and neglect all else.'

l. 165. The Seven Giants are the Seven Deadly Sins.

l. 169. Peaked shoes had excessively long toes, and were considered very fashionable.

l. 176. 'Dismembering' God by swearing by parts of His body was common in the Middle Ages. Chaucer's Pardoner deplores precisely the same oaths, ' "By Goddes precious herte" and "By His nayles." ' There are instances where the 'nails' refer to the nails driven into the Cross. But it seems likely that in the passage from Chaucer and that from Langland the poets would have had the fingernails in mind on account of the juxtaposition of another part of the body — the heart.

l. 200. 'So long as you give up the study of logic.' Logic, with Grammar and Rhetoric, made up the Trivium — the first three liberal arts studied in Medieval Schools.

St. Francis, in consonance with his plans for the utter humility of the friars, intended that they should not be learned. This contrasts with the ideas of St. Dominic. (*Vide* J. R. H. Moorman, *Church Life in England in the 13th Century*, p. 368.)

l. 206. *Qui numerat, etc.*: Psalm cxlvi. 4 (Vulg.), cxlvii. 4 (A.V.).

l. 214. The charters of religious houses specified the number of inmates who were to inhabit them.

l. 227. *Non concupisces, etc.*: Exodus xx. 17.

l. 231. The penance enjoined by parish priests made the people ashamed of sin; but the friars undercut them by offering penance without tears. Cf. Chaucer's Friar Huberd for an identical picture:

> For he hadde power of confessioun,
> As seyde hymself, moore than a curat . . .
> Ful swetely herde he confessioun,
> And plesaunt was his absolucioun . . .
> Therfore in stede of wepynge and preyeres
> Men moote yeve silver to the povre freres.
>   (*General Prologue*, ll. 208 *et seq.*)

Indeed, Friar Huberd and Friar Flatterer have almost every-thing in common in both their very unpleasant characters. See also note on l. 134 of Section II of the present edition.

l. 233. **as** = just as. Westminster, cf. l. 83 in this section.

l. 239. i.e. Executors of wills give part of the deceased man's hard-earned money to the friars, and then pocket the remainder.

l. 249. 'Conscience and Hypocrisy had a hard struggle.'

l. 257. **redde quod debes**: Matthew xviii. 28.

l. 270. **but if dette lette it**: This refers back to *redde quod debes*, in l. 257. 'Pay back what you owe' implies 'make restitution for misdeeds by penance'.

l. 274. **a lord**: i.e. a bishop. Cf. note on l. 649 of Section II.

l. 284. i.e. 'It is only with difficulty that they will recover.'

l. 289. **Penetrans domos**: Skeat notes that this alludes 'to the text "Ex his enim sunt, qui *penetrant domos*, et captiuas ducunt mulierculas oneratas peccatis, quae ducuntur uariis desideriis" (2 Timothy iii. 6).'

l. 291. **conne somme crafte**: cf. l. 156, above.

l. 295. **limitour**: *vide* note on l. 138 of Section II.

l. 313. Cf. note on l. 134 of Section II.

l. 316. The reference is to 'conventual letters' which were charters given to anyone who could afford them, and which entitled him or her to honorary membership of one of the Orders of Friars. Thus, the purchaser was automatically represented in the prayers and good deeds of the Brother-hood.

l. 330. '. . . and walk to the ends of the earth in search of Piers the Ploughman. For he can destroy Pride, and find an honest livelihood for these Friars who live by flattery and set them-selves against me. Now may Nature avenge me, and send me His help and healing, until I have found Piers the Plough-man. Then he cried aloud for Grace . . .' (J. F. Goodridge, *Piers the Ploughman, Translated into Modern English*).

l. 333. **Kynde me avenge**: Refers back to l. 154.

Thus the circular pattern of the poem is formed. Once again the individual conscience searches for the good life — Piers the Ploughman — just as it did at the beginning of the poem. But it is a very different man who now stands firmly on the side of Truth; it is a man who has learned that any hope of finding God except by love alone is doomed to failure. Personally humiliated, and with all the world against him, he has, paradoxically, never been so confident, for now he knows that one skill only is required to find Truth: 'Lerne to love,' quod Kynde, 'and leve of all othre.' The Easter vision had shown him perfect Love made manifest — Love who would suffer and die for Truth's sake. But he sees now that Easter was not a matter of once for all. For every man, life is a pilgrimage to find Piers the Plough-man; the struggle of Conscience and Antichrist continues for all time:

> And the Son of Man was not crucified once for all,
> The blood of the martyrs not shed once for all,
> The lives of the Saints not given once for all:
> But the Son of Man is crucified always
> And there shall be Martyrs and Saints.
> And if blood of Martyrs is to flow on the steps
> We must first build the steps;
> And if the Temple is to be cast down
> We must first build the Temple.

(T. S. Eliot, from The Rock)

Glossary

The following abbreviations have been used:

adj.	– adjective	past part.	– past participle
adv.	– adverb	pl.	– plural
conj.	– conjunction	poss.	– possessive
gen.	– genitive	prep.	– preposition
imper.	– imperative	pres. part.	– present participle
interj.	– interjection	pron.	– pronoun
N.	– Note	Sec.	– Section
n.	– noun	v.	– verb

a (adj. and prep.), one, one single, in, on

abedde (adv.), to bed

ablende (v.), blind

ableynte (v.), blinded

aboughte (v. past part.), paid for

abye (v.), pay for

ac (conj.), but

accidie (n.), sloth, see N. Sec. II, l. 392

acombred (v. past part.), overcome

acomptes (n.), accounts

acorden (v.), agree

acorse (v.), curse

addre (n.), serpent

adradde (adj.), greatly afraid

aferd (v. past part.), frightened

afere (v.), frighten away

afereth (v.), terrifies

affaiten (v.), tame

affrayned (v.), asked

afor (prep.), before

after (prep.), according to, for, in addition, after

agein (prep.), against, in return for

ageines (adv.), back, again

ageyne (conj.), before the time that

agrounde (adv.), aground, on earth

akale (v. past part.), chilled

al (adj. and pron.), all

al-arme (interj.), to arms

ale (n.), ale-house

alkin, alkyn (adj.), of every kind

alowde (adv.), loudly

als (adv. and conj.), also

amende (v.), repair

amendement (n.), amendment of life, betterment

amendes (n.), amends; **to amendes,** as satisfaction for

ampulles (n.), see N. Sec. II, l. 527

an (conj. and prep.), and, on

ancres (n.), anchorites
and (conj.), and, if
anon (adv.), at once
apewarde (n.), ape-keeper
appayre (v.), harm, diminish
appeltre (n.), appletree
appendeth (v.), belongs
appertly (adv.), clearly, plainly
apposed (v.), questioned
ar (adv.), before
arest (adv.), at rest, asleep
armes (n.), arms, coat of arms
arn, arne (v.), are
arrayen (v.), prepare
arrere (adv.), backwards
arst (adv.), first
arwes (n.), arrows
asketh (v.), requires
aspie (v.), see, discover
assaye (v.), try
asseled (v.), sealed
assoile ⎱ (v.), absolve
assoilen ⎰
asswage (v.), assuage
atamede (v.), opened
ateynte (v. past part.), accused
athynketh (v.), grieves, repents
attached (v.), arrested, claimed
atte (prep.), at the
aughte (pron.), anything, everything
auncere (n.), a Danish steel-yard, i.e. weighing machine
auntred (v.), ventured
auntrous (adj. and n.) adventurous (people), knights adventurers
auter (n.), altar

aventure (n.), chance
awayted (v.), watched
awaytestow (v.), are you watching?
awreke (v.), avenge
axed (v.), asked
axeth (v.), asks, desires
ay (adv.), always, continually

babeled (v.), muttered
baberlipped (adj.), thick-lipped
bachelers, see N. Sec. I, l. 87
bacoun (n.), bacon
bad (v.), commanded
bagge (n.), bag, money-bag
bakbitynge (n.), slander
baldly (adv.), boldly
bale (n.), sorrow
baleised (v.), beaten with a rod
balled (adj.), bald
banne (v.), curse
bar (v.), carried
baren (v.), carried, took
bareyne (adj.), barren
barfote (adj.), bare-foot
barn, barne (n.), child, man
barre (n.), bar
baudy (adj.), dirty
baxsteres (n.), bakers (probably female)
be (prep.), by; (v.), be
beches (n.), beeches
bede (v.), commanded
bedes (n.), beads, rosary
beggeres (n.), beggars
behote (v.), made vows
belye (v.), slander
be-mente (v.), signified
ben (v.), be, are
benfait (n.), benefit

benygne (adj.), kind
berde (n.), beard
bere (v.), bore
bereth (v.), carries
beryng (n.), bearing
bestes (n.), beasts
bete (v.), beat
beth (v.), are
Bethleem (n.), Bethlehem
Beton (n.), pet name for Beatrice
Bette (n.), a man's name (perhaps from Bartholomew)
bette (adj. and adv.), better
beupere (n.), reverend father (applied to monks and friars)
bi (prep.), by, according to, with regard to, about
bi so (conj.) provided that
bicche (n.), bitch
bicome (v.), became, went
bidde (v.), pray
bidders (n.), beggars
biddyng (n.), commands
biden (v.), await
bidraveled (v.), slobbered, made greasy
bidyng (adj.), persistent
bifalleth (v.), belongs, happens
bigge (v.), buy
bigiled (v.), beguiled
biheste (n.), promise
bihoveth (v.), is necessary
bihyghte (v.), promised
bi-japed (v.), mocked
bikere (v.), contend
biknowe (v.), acknowledge, confess
bileve (n.), belief, creed; (v.), believe

binethe (prep.), beneath
biquashte (v.), fell in pieces
biseche (v.), pray, beg, implore
biseged (v.), besieged
bisette (v.), employ, use, arrange
biseye (v.), visited
bisi (adj.), busy
bislabered (adj.), beslobbered
bismer (n.), reviling, detraction
biswonke (v.), gained by work
bit (v.), commands
bitelbrowed (adj.), with beetling brows
bitter (n.), bitterness
bitwene (prep.), between
bityde (v.), betide, happen
bityme (adv.), soon
blased (v.), shone brightly
blasen (n.), coat of arms
blede (v.), bleed
blent (v.), blinded
blered (adj. and v.), bleared, made misty
blissed (adj. and v. past part.), blessed, truly holy
blode (n.), blood
blosmed (v.), blossomed
blustreden (v.), wandered about
blynde (adj.), blind
bocches (n.), tumours
bochere (n.), butcher
boke (n.), book, Bible
boldeliche (adv.), boldly
bolke (n.), belch
bolle (n.), bowl, drinking bowl
bolneth (v.), swells
bonched (v.), struck, knocked

bonde (v.), bound up

bondman, bondemen (n.), agricultural labourer(s)

bore (v.), born

bores (n.), boars

borghe (n.), surety, pledge

bornes (n.), stream's

borwe (v.), borrow

borwes (n.), sureties, god-parents

borwgh (n.), surety, pledge

bosted, y-bosted (v.), boasted

bote (n.), benefit

bote (v.), bit

botelees (adj.), without remedy

boteles (adj.), without boots

bothe (adj., adv. and pron.), both; (adv.), also

botheres (pron.), of both of them

boure (n.), inner room (usually of ladies)

bow (n.), branch

boxome (adj.), obedient, humble, gentle

boy (n.), young man, servant. Often used contemptuously.

breche (n.), breeches

bred (n.), bread

breke (v.), should break, break

brennyng (v. pres. part.), burning

brent (adj.), burnished, burnt

breth (n.), breath

brevet (n.), letter of indulgence

brewestere (n.), brewer (probably female)

breyde (v.), hastened

bribours (n.), robbers

brief (n.), authorising letter

broche (v.), pierce

brockes (n.), badgers

brocour, brocoure (n.), broker, an authorised maker of bargains

brode (adj.), broad, wide

broke (adj.), torn, tattered

brouke (v.), enjoy, receive

browe (v. past part.), brewed

buirde (n.), lady, maiden

buirn (n.), man

bummed (v.), tasted

burdoun (n.), pilgrim's staff

burgeis, burgeyses (n.), townspeople

but, but if (conj.), but, unless

buxome, see **boxome**

buyrn (n.), man

byfel (v.), happened

byhihte (v.), promised

byles (n.), boils

bymeneth (v.), signifies

bytokeneth (v.), signifies

cacche (v.), catch, receive, take

cacchepolle (n.), minor officer

caityve (n.), wretch

cam (v.), came

can (v.), know, am able

canoun (n.), canon law

caple (n.), horse

cardiacles (n.), heart attacks, spasms

cardinales (adj.), cardinal (virtues), see Sec. I, l. 104 where it implies derivation from Latin *cardo*, hinge

carefullich (adv.), sadly, anxiously

Caro (n. Latin), flesh, see N. Sec. III, l. 169
carpe (v.), spoke
caste (v.), planned
castel (n.), castle
casten (v.), decided
casteth (v.), make
catel (n.), goods, wealth
caudel (n.), mess
caught, caught of (v.), received
caurimaury (n.), rough cloth
Caym (n.), Cain
caytyves (n.), wretches
Cesaris (n.), Caesar's
cesse (v.), cease
chaced (v.), hurried
chaffare (n.), trade
chalanged (v.), accused
chalangynge (n.), accusing
chalengen, see N. Sec. I, l. 93
chapelleynes (n.), chaplain's
chapitelhous (n.), chapter house
chapitere (n.), chapter of the convent
chapman, chapmen (n.), merchant(s)
chasten (v.), discipline
cheke (n.), cheek
cheker (n.), exchequer
chele (n.), cold
Chepe (n.), Cheapside (London)
chere (n.), face, expression
cherlis (n.), people of evil behaviour, serfs
chese (n.), cheese; (v.), chose
chesibles (n.), chasubles
cheven (v.), prosper

chevesances (n.), agreements about money loans
cheytif (adj.), humble, wretched
chiere (n.), expression
chieve (v.), prosper
chirityme (n.), cherrytime (see Gen. Introd., p. xv)
chivaler (n.), knight
chiveled (v.), trembled, shivered
chose, y-chose (v.), chosen
chyde (v.), quarrel
chydynge (n.), quarrelling
chyn (n.), chin
clameth, claymeth (v.), claims, claims the right (to hear it)
civile (n.), civil law
cleargealy (adv.), in a clerkly manner
clef (v.), split
clene (adj.), pure
clereliche (adv.), entirely, clearly
clerke (adj.), scholarly, clerical
clerkes (n.), scholars, priests
clippe (v.), seize, **clippe we**, let us embrace
clips (n.), eclipse
closeth (v.), encloses, shuts, buries
cnowest (v.), knowest
cofre (n.), coffer, chest
cokes (n.), cooks
combraunce (n.), trouble
comsed (v.), began
comsynge (n.), beginning
comunes (n.), common people, provisions

conne (v.), know, learn

conseille (n.), council, secret, advice; (v.), advise

consistorie (n.), ecclesiastical court

constable (n.), warden

contenaunce (n.), outward show, looks, favour, favour of someone's confiding

contrarieth (v.), oppose

contre (n.), country

contrepleteth (v.), oppose

contreved (v.), devised

cope (n.), cope, cape; (v.), **cope us**, provide ourselves with copes

copis (n.), copes, capes worn by friars

corseint (n.), saint

coste (n.), region

cosyn (n.), cousin

cote (n.), coat

coudestow? (v.), couldest thou?

coupe (n.), guilt

couped, y-couped (v.), cut, see N. Sec. III, l. 217

courbed (v.), knelt down

couthe (v.), knew, understood, could, make known

coveiten (v.), desire

covenaunte (n.), condition, agreement

covent (n.), convent

coventes (n.), convent's, friary's

coveytise (n.), covetousness, greed, chief desire

crafte (n.), trade, skill

crepynge (adj.), creeping

cristene (n.), Christians

croft (n.), enclosed field

croppe (n.), tree-top

croune (n.), crown

crounyng (n.), tonsure

cruche (n.), cross

crystene (adj.), Christian

culle (v.), kill

cuntre (n.), country, district

cupmel (n.), a measure of a cup, see N. Sec. II, l. 225

curatoures (n.), curates

cure (n.), cure of souls

curteisye (n.), courtesy, manners

cusse (v.), kiss

dagge (v.), cut, see N. Sec. IV, l. 93

damaiseles (n.), maidens

dame (n.), lady, mother

dampne (v.), damn

dar (v.), dare

daunce (v.), dance

dawe (v.), dawn

debate (n.), strife

decretales (n.), decretals, collections of popes' edicts, etc.

ded (n.), the dead

dede (n.), deed; (v.), did

dedes (n.), deeds, legal documents

defaute (n.), lack, default

defence (n.), prohibition

defien, defye (v.), digest, be digested

del (n.), deal, amount

dele (n.), part, amount, share; (v.), have dealings

delitable (adj.), delightful

delveres (n.), diggers

demen (v.), judge, decide

departable (adj.), distinct, separable

depe (adj.), deep; (adv.), deeply

deprave (v.), slander

dere (adj.), dear, beloved; (v.), harm

derke (adj.), dark

derworth (adj.), precious

despended (v.), spent, used

descryve (v.), describe, name

destruye (v.), destroy, waste

deth-yvel (n.), death-drink

dette (n.), debt

devors (n.), divorce

devyse (v.), plan

deye (v.), die

diapenidion (n.), see N. Sec. II, l. 123

discreve (v.), describe

dissheres (n.), dish-seller (female)

do (v.), do, compel; **do me,** place myself; **ydo,** completed

doctour (n.), doctor, teacher

doel (n.), lamentation

dogge (n.), dog

doke (n.), duck

dome (n.), judgement; **Heygh Dome,** Day of Judgement

domesday, Doomsday (n.), The Day of Judgement

don, done (v.), cause, force, make

dones (n. gen.), of kind; **what dones man,** what kind of man

donet (n.), primer, see N. Sec. II, l. 209

dore (n.), door

dorste (v.), dared

doughtier (adj.), more brave

doughtilich (adv.), bravely

doune (prep.), down; **doune right,** entirely; **up so doune,** upside down

doust (n.), dust

dozeine (adj.), dozen

dragges (n.), drugs

draperes (n.), drapers

dredden (v.), feared

drede (n. or v.), dread, fear

dredfully (adv.), in terror, fearfully

drewery (n.), precious thing, treasure, object of affection

drowe (v.), drew, betook, made (one's) way

drowgh (v.), approached

dryven (v.), spend, pass, force, drive

dryvende (v. pres. part.), driving, dashing

duk (n.), duck

dure (v.), last

dureth (v.), lasts, endures

dyas (n.), medicines

dykers (n.), ditchers

dyne (n.), din; (v.), dine, take a meal

dynte (n.), blow

eche (adj.), each; **eche a,** so also

edefye (v.), build

edwite (v.), rebuke, scold

eet (v.), eat

eft (adv.), again

eftsones (adv.), soon after, again

egged (v.), incited

elde (n.), age, old age

eller (n.), elder tree

elles, ellis (adv.), other times, otherwise, else

enbawmed (v.), anointed

enfourmed (v.), taught

engyned (v.), contrived

Engelonde (n.), England

enjoigne (v.), enjoin, bid

ennuyed (v.), annoyed, troubled

ensample (n.), example

entysynge (n.), temptation

envye (n.), envy, spite

er (adv.), before

eres (n.), ears

eried (v.), ploughed

Ermonye (n.), Armenia

ers (n.), backside

erye (v.), plough

eschaunges (n.), barterings

ese (n.), ease

est (adj. and n.), east

eten (v.), eat

evele (adv.), ill, badly

evel-ytaughte (adj.), ill-mannered

even (n.), evening

evene (adv.), squarely

evene-cristene (n.), fellow Christians

evre (adv.), always

eyghen, eyen (n.), eyes

eyther (pron.), each

faire (adv.), plainly, kindly; (n.), fair. See N. Sec. II, l. 328

fairy (n.), enchantment

falleth (v.), falls, belongs, befits

fals (n.), falsehood

falshed (n.), falsehood; **falshed of fastyng,** breaking vows of fasting

fange (v.), take, receive

fantasies (n.), fantastic stories

fare (n.), business, stir

faren (v.), gone, travelled

fareth (v.), happens

faste (adv.), tightly

faucones (n.), falcons

fayteden (v.), begged deceitfully

fecche (v.), fetch, bring back

feire (adv.), fortunately

feith (n.), faith

fel (n.), skin

felawes (n.), companions, companion's (refers to Eve in Sec. III, l. 399)

felde (n.), field

fele (v.), feel

feledest (v.), felt

felle (adj.), cruel

felly (adv.), fiercely

feloun (n.), criminal

felyng (n.), touch

fende (n.), devil

fendekynes (n.), little fiends

fenestre (n.), window

fer (adj. and adv.), far

ferde (v.), acted, seemed

feres (n.), companions

ferly (n.), wonder, marvel, strange happening

fernyere (adv.), in times past, formerly

ferther (adv.), further

fette (v.), fetched, produced

fevres (n.), fevers

feynen (v.), imagine

feyntise (n.), faintness, weakness

fieble (adj.), weak

file (n.), daughter, mistress, see N. Sec. II, l. 160

firses (n.), sprigs of a furze bush

flatte (v.), threw

fleen (v.), flee

flegh (v.), fly, avoid, flee

fleigh (v.), fled

flesshe (n.), flesh

flex (n.), flax

fluxe (n.), flux, flow

fode (n.), food

foles, folis (n.), fools; **foles hem maketh,** make themselves out to be fools

folwar (n.), follower

folweth (v.), follows

fonde (v.), found, discovered, provided for

fonded (v.), tried

foon (n.), enemies

forbete (v.), beat down, enfeeble

fordo, fordon (v.), destroy, ruin

forejoures (n.), messengers, harbingers

forfadres (n.), forefathers

forgaf (v.), granted

forred (adj.), fur-trimmed

forsake (v.), deny

forsleuthed (v.), wasted in idleness

forsleves (n.), fronts of the sleeves

for-thi (conj.), therefore

forto (conj.), in order to

forwandred (v.), exhausted by wandering

forweny (v.), pamper

forwit (n.), foreknowledge, foresight

forward (n.), agreement

foryete (v.), forget, forgotten

fote (n.), foot

foule (adj.), foul, wicked; (adv.), **-ly, -ly**

foules (n.), fowls, birds

fourmed (v.), formed, prepared

fourlonge (n.), furlong

frained, frayned (v.), asked

fram (prep.), from

fraunchise (m.), freedom

fre (adj.), freeborn, free, generous

freke (n.), man

frendes (n.), friends

frenesyes (n.), fits of madness

frere (n.), friar

fresche (adj.), fresh

frette (v.), ate

fritth (n.), forest

fro (prep.), from

frokke (n.), gown, frock, habit

frute (n.), fruit

furst (adj. and adv.), first

fyn (adj.), fine, clever

fynd (v.), provide for

fyndyng (n.), living

fysyke (n.), medicine

fyve (adj.), five

gabbynges (n.), lies

gadelyng (n.), vagabond

gadereth (v.), collects money

Galice (n.), Galicia

galoches (n.), see N. Sec. III, l. 217

galoun (n.), gallon
gan (v.), did
gardyner (n.), gardener
garnements (n.), garments, clothes
gart (v.), caused
Gascoigne (n.), Gascony
gat (v.), begot, conceived
gate (n.), gate, way, walking
geaunt (n.), giant
gentrice (n.), noble nature
gerelande (n.), garland
gerlis (n.), children (of either sex)
gert (v.), caused
gesse (n.), guesswork
gete (v.), get
geven (v.), gave
gilte (adj.), golden
girt (v.), threw
gladye (v.), delight
glasen (adj.), glass
glede (n.), burning coal, spark
glee (n.), singing
glewmannes (n.), gleeman's, minstrel's
globbed, y-globbed (v.), gulped down
glose (n.), commentary, The Glosa Ordinaria
glosed, y-glosed (v.), explained
gloseth (v.), interprets falsely, deceives
glosynges (n.), deceits
glotonye, glotoun (n.), gluttony, a glutton
gode, goed (adj.), good
gome (n.), man
gon (v.), go; **y-go** (v.), gone
goodis (n.), goods

gossib (n.), neighbour, friend
gost, goste (n.), spirit
goth (v.), goes
gothely (v.), gurgle, rumble
gowe (v.), let us go
gradde (v.), cried aloud
graffe (v.), graft
gramercy (n.), thank you very much
graunge (n.), grange, (abbey) farm
graythely (adv.), quickly, duly
gree (n.), prize
gret, grete (v.), weep
grete (adj.), large, great
grette (v.), greeted
gretter (adj.), greater
greve (v.), grieve
gris (n.), pigs
grome (n.), groom
gropeth (v.), feel, touch
grote (n.), groat, i.e. a silver 4d. piece
grounde (n.), ground, reason
grym (adj.), grim, heavy
gult (n.), guilt
gunne (v.), began
gutte (n.), belly, gut
gyaunts (n.), giants
Gybbe (n.), (abbreviation for) Gilbert
gyde (n.), guide
gyle (n.), guile, deceit
gyled (v.), deceived
gylours (n.), deceivers
gylti (adj.), guilty
gynne (n.), engine
gynnynge (n.), beginning
gyoure (n.), guide, leader
gyved (v.), fettered

haberjoun (n.), coat of mail

habite (n.), clothing

hagge (n.), hag

hailse (v.), greet

hakeneyman (n.), horse dealer, one who lets out horses for hire

haliday (n.), holyday

halidom (n.), saintly relics

halt (v.), holds

halve (n.), half

han (v.), have

hansel (n.), prepayment; to hansel, as a propitiation, as a bribe

happe (n.), fortune, success

hardliche (adv.), boldly

hardyer (adv.), more boldly

harlotes (n.), rascals', of indecent story tellers

harlotrie (n.), crude story, dissipation

harpeden (v.), played harps

harrow (interj.), alas

hastow?(v. singular), have you?

hat, hatte (v.), is called

hatte (n.), hat

haukes (n.), hawk's

have (v.), have, take

hed (n.), head, headdress

hede (n.), heed

heed (n.), head

heel (n.), health

heep (n.), crowd

heet (v.), commanded

hegge (n.), hedge

heighe (adj.), high, proud

hele (n.), health; (v.), keep, conceal

helme (n.), helmet

helynge (v. pres. part.), healing

hem (pron.), them, themselves, for themselves

hem-self (pron.), see Sec. I, l. 117, 'for all of them'

hende (adj.), polite, courteous

hendeliche (adv.), courteously

hendenesse (n.), courtesy

hende-speche (n.), courteous speech

hennes (adv.), hence, from here

hent, hente (v.), seized

heo (pron.), she

hep (n.), heap, crowd

her, here (pron.), their, of them

heraud (n.), herald (refers to Abraham in Sec. III, l. 81)

herberwed (v.), lodged

herde (v.), heard

here (v.), hear

here-of (adv.), about it, about this

herfor (adv.), for this reason

hernes (n.), corners

herte (n.), heart

het (v.), commanded

heved (n.), head

heveneriche (n. gen.), of the kingdom of heaven

hevy (adj.), heavy, sad

hevynesse (n.), sadness

hewe (n.), servant

heygh (adj.), high; Heygh Dome, Day of Judgement

heyre (n.), hair-shirt

hider (adv.), hither

hiegh, hieghe (adj.), high; the hieghe name, God's name

hieghnesse (n.), courage

hight (v.), commended

highte (v.), commanded

hii (pron.), they

hippyng (v. pres. part.), hopping, skipping

hir, hire (pron.), her, their

hise (pron.), his

hitte (v.), hit, struck, threw down

hode (n.), hood

hoked (adj.), hooked

hokkerye (n.), door-to-door selling

holden (v.), keep, kept to; **y-holden**, esteemed, considered

hole (adj.), whole

holiwrit (n.), Scriptures

holwe (adj.), hollow

hondes (n.), hands

hondreth (adj.), hundred

honged (v.), hanged

hoore (adj.), white-headed

hope (v.), consider, imagine

hore (adj.), white-headed

ho-so (pron.), whoso, whoever

hostellere (n.), inn-keeper

hostrye (n.), inn

hote (adj.), hot; (v.), command; **yhote** (v. past part.), named

housbonderye (n.), thrift

houve (n.), hood, see also N. Sec. IV, l. 122

hoved (v.), waited about

hudde (v.), hid

huire (n.), wages

hulpe (v.), helped

hulles (n.), hills

hungriliche (adv.), hungrily

hyden (v.), hide

hyed (v.), hurried

hyghte (v.), commanded

hym-selven (pron.), himself

hyne (n.), servant

hyre (n.), payment

ich, ik (pron.), I; **so the ik,** so may I thrive

ilke (adj.), same; (n.), very thing, one thing

ille (adv.), badly, wickedly; (n.), evil

ilyke (adj.), like, same

i-made (v. preterite), made

ingonge (n.), entrance

inowe (adj.), enough

inparfit (adj.), imperfect

inpugnen (v.), impugn, call in question

jangelers (n.), smutty chatterers

jangelynge (n.), gossip, quarrelling, crude chattering

japed (v.), tricked

japers (n.), jesters

joutes (n.), soups, broths

jugged (v.), rode swiftly

juste, justes (n.), jousting, tournament; (v.), joust, tilt

Juwen (n. gen. pl.), of the Jews; (adj.), Jewish

kairen (v.), wander, make one's way

kare (n.), care, anxiety

kayseres (n.), emperors

kene (adj.), sharp, bitter, bold

kenne (v.), teach

kepen (v.), guard

kepere (n.), guardian

keure (v.), recover
kichyne (n.), kitchen
kidde (v.), showed
kirke (n.), church
kirtel (n.), underjacket
knaves (n.), boys, servants
knele (v.), kneel
knowes (n.), knees
knowleched (v.), acknowledged, confessed
knyf (n.), knife
kokewolde (n.), cuckold
kourteby (n.), short coat
kullen (v.), kill
kut (v.), cut
kychyne (n.), kitchen
kynde (adj.), natural; (n.), people, nature; **Kynde Wytte**, common sense
kyndeli, kyndelich, kyndely (adv.), naturally, simply, in simple terms
kyng (n.), king
kyngriche (n.), kingdom
kynne (n.), kindred
kynnes (n. gen.), kind of, sort of
kyrke (n.), church

lacche (v.), catch, take
lacchyng (n.), receiving, taking
ladde (v.), led
laft (v.), left
lakke (v.), find fault with
lape (v.), lap
largelich (adv.), fully
Largenesse (n.), Bounty, Generosity
lasse (adv.), less
lat, late (v.), let, let me

latro, see N. Sec. II, l. 484
laught (v.), took
lecchoure (n.), lecher, lustful person
leche (n.), doctor
lechecrafte (n.), medical skill
lede (n.), man; (v.), govern, carried
leef (adj.), dear, beloved, pleased; (n.), leaf, see also N. Sec. II, l. 203
leep (v.), leapt
leest (adj.), least
legge (v.), pledge
legioun (n.), legion, large number
leke (n.), leek
lele (adj.), true, loyal, faithful
lelest (adj.), most true
lelly (adv.), loyally, faithfully
leme (n.), brightness
lemman (n.), lover
lene (v.), lend, give to
lene (adj.), lean
lened (v.), leaned
lenger (adj.), longer
lenten (n.), Lent, see N. Sec. III, l. 208
lentestow ? (v.), lentest thou? i.e. didst thou lend?
leodes (n.), men, people
lepe (v.), leap, run. In Sec. II, l. 483 is ref. to nickname 'landleaper' for a pilgrim
lere (n.), face; **A loveli ladi of lere,** a lady of lovely countenance
lered (adj.), educated (hence (n.) 'educated men')
leren (v.), teach
les (v.), lost, forfeited

L

lese (v.), lose

lessoun (n.), lesson

leste (adj.), least; (conj.), lest

lesynge (n.), loss, losses, lies, lying stories

lete (v.), cease, leave off, permit, allow, consider

letheren (adj.), leather

lette (v.), prevent, delay

letter (n.), hinderer, preventer

letterure (n.), learning

lettynge (n.), delay

leute (n.), loyalty, loyal subjects

leve (adj.), dear; (n.), permission; (v.), believe, leave

lever, levere (adj. and adv.), dearer, sooner, rather, preferably

leves (n.), leaves

lewed (adj.), ignorant, 'lay' as opposed to the learned 'clerical'

lewte (n.), loyalty, uprightness

leye, y-leye (v.), lain

leyth (v.), lays, places

libben (v.), live

libbyng (v. pres. part.), living

liche (adv.), like

lif (n.), life, person

lifdayes (n.), days of (one's) life

liflode (n.), food

ligge (v.), lie, reside

lighter (adj.), easier

likam (n.), body

likerous (adj.), pleasing to the senses

liketh (v.), pleases

likth (v.), lies, speaks falsely

limitoures (n.), limiters, see N. Sec. II, l. 138

lisse (n.), joy

liste (n.), edge of cloth, strip of cloth; (v.), desire

listres (n.), lectors, see N. Sec. II, l. 138

lith (n.), limb, body; (v.), lies, remains, resides

lither (adj.), wicked

lixte (v.), lie, tell lies

lobyes (n.), lubbers, idle loafers

loft (n.), sky, height, in Sec. III, l. 248.

loke (v.), look, take note

loked (v.), gazed, looked

lombe (n.), lamb

lomer (adv.), more often

lond (n.), land, field

lone (n.), loan

longeth (v.), belong

loo (interj.), behold!

lopen (v.), leaped

lordeynes (n.), fools, blockheads

lore (n.), teaching

lore, y-lore (v.), lost

lorel (n.), wretch, worthless fellow

loseles (n.), scoundrels

loth (adj.), unwilling, loath

Loth (n.), Lot

lotyeth (v.), lurk

louke (v.), lock, enclose

loupen (v.), leapt, fled

lourynge (v. pres. part.), scowling, looking sullen

lousi (adj.), lousy

lovedayes, see N. Sec. II, l. 427

loveli, loveliche (adj.), lovely, pleasant

lovye (v.), love

low (adj.), meek, humble

lowe (v.), didst tell falsely

lowen (on) (v.), lied (against)

lowgh (v.), laughed

Lumbardes (n.), Lombards, see N. Sec. II, l. 242

lusard (n.), lizard

luste (v.), desired, (it) pleased

luted (v.), played on a lute

luther (adj.), wicked, ill-tempered

lyard (n.), grey horse, see N. Sec. III, l. 126

lybbeth (v.), live

lye (v.), lie

lyer (n.), liar

lyeth (v.), lies, deceives

lyf (n.), life

lyflode (n.), food

lyges (n.), subjects, liegemen

lyghter (adj.), lighter, easier

lyghtlych (adv.), easily

lykam (n.), body

lykyng (n.), wish, desire, pleasure

lyme (n.), limb

lynnen (n.), linen

lyppe (n.), portion

lys (n.), lice

lyser (n.), edge of cloth

lyven (v.), live

maistres (n.), lords, learned men; maistres Freres, master friars; see also N. Sec. I, l. 87

males (n.), bags

mamely (v.), prate, preach

manere (adj.), kind of, sort of; (n.), manor, estate

manlyche (n.), charitable, generous

mansed (adj.), excommunicated

manye (adj.), many

marchandise (n.), merchandise, wares

marche (n.), province

marke (n.), a mark, i.e. coin then worth 13/4d.

mase (n.), confused mass of people

masse (n.), mass

matere (n.), matter

matynes (n.), matins

maugre (prep.), in spite of

maundement (n.), commandment

mawe (n.), maw, stomach

maydenes (n.), maidens, virgins

mayne (n.), power

mayntene (v.), support

mayntenaunce (n.), maintenance, conniving at misdoings

maystrye (n.), mastery, power

medle (v.), fight

megre (adj.), thin

meke (v.), humble

mele (n.), meal

melke (n.), milk

membre (n.), limb

mene (adj.), poor; (n.), a medium; (v.), signify (also in phrase to mene)

mened (reflex. v.), complained

mennes (n.), men's, people's

menynge (n.), meaning, token

menyvere (n.), miniver, fur

mercere (n.), mercer

merciable (adj.), merciful

mercy (v.), thank you, pardon

merke (adj.), dark; (n.), heed, note

merkenesse (n.), darkness

merveille (n.), marvel, wonder

merveilouse (adj.), wonderful

meschaunce (n.), misfortune

messe (n.), mass

mesurable (adj.), reasonable, moderate

mesure (n.), moderation

mete (n.), meat, meal; (v.), measure, meet

meten (v.), dream

meynpernoure (n.), one who stands bail for another, surety

meynprise (n.), bail, security

mitagacioun (n.), mercy

mite (n.), mite; **a mite,** in the least

mo (adv.), more

moche (adj. and adv.), great, greatly

mochel (adj.), great, much

moder (n.), mother

modicum (n. Latin), scarcity

molde (n.), earth, world

momme (n.), small sound, 'a single word'

montaigne (n.), mountain

monyals (n.), nuns

moo (adv.), more

moste (adj.), greatest; (v.), must

mote (v.), may, must

mouthed (v.), spoke

mowe (v.), may, can

Moyses (n.), Moses

murthes (n.), entertainments

myckel (adj.), great

myd (prep.), with

myghte (n.), power, strength

myne (pron.), mine

mynours (n.), miners

myrthe (n.), happiness, joy

myrye (adj.), merry

mysdo (v.), maltreat, done wrong

myseise (n.), pain, discomfort; **for myseise,** to counteract discomfort

myssayde (v.), slandered, insulted, rebuked

myste (n.), mist

myte (n.), mite; **a mite,** in the least

namelich, namely (adv.), particularly

nappe (v.), sleep, fall asleep

naught (adv.), not

ne (adv. and conj.), nor, not

nede (n.), need; **at nede,** in time of need

nedeler (n.), needle seller

nedes (adv.), of necessity, necessarily

nedful (adj.), needful

nedle (n.), needle

nedy (adj.), poor, needy (used also as a noun)

neghed (v.), drew close

neighen (v.), approach

nel, nelle (v.), will not

nempne (v.), name

nere (prep.), near; (v.), might not be; **yif thei nere,** if they did not exist

neyghe (prep.), near

niegh (adv.), near

nil (v.), will not; **nil naughte**, will not

nippe (n.), cold region

noble (n.), gold coin valued 6/8*d*.

nolde (v.), would not

none other (pron.), nothing else

nones (n.), mid-day meal

nonne (n.), nun; **to nonne**, who is a nun

nought (adv.), not; (pron.), nothing

noumbre (n.), number

noumpere (n.), umpire

noyther (conj.), neither; **ne noyther ?** nor is there?

nymmeth (v. imper.), take !

nys (v.), is not

nyvelynge (v. pres. part.), snivelling

o (adj.), one

obrode (adv.), abroad, far out, broadly

of (adv.), off; (prep.), of

of-raughte (v.), extended; **the people that of-raughte**, that extended to (or affected) the people

okes (n.), oak trees

on (adj.), one; (prep.), in

one (adj.), alone

ones, onis (adv.), once

onlich (adv.), only

oon (adj.), one

ordeigned (v.), ordained, laid down

orgonye (n.), organ music

Oseye (n.), Alsace

other (conj.), or, otherwise

otherwhile(s) (adv.), sometimes

oughte (pron.), everything, something, anything

oures (n.), hours (in the breviary), i.e. service times

overdelicatly (adv.), too luxuriously

over-hoveth (v.), hovers over

over-seye (v.), overlooked; **over-seye me**, forgot myself

overtilte (v.), overturned

owre (adj.), our

Pacience (n.), Patience

pak-nedle (n.), packing-needle

paleys (n.), palace

palmers, see N. Sec. II, l. 527

palsye (n.), palsy

paltok (n.), jacket, cloak

pans (n.), pennies

paradys (n.), Paradise

parcel (n.), part, share

parceyved (v.), perceived, understood

pare (v.), clip

parfourned (v.), performed

parled (v.), spoken

paroschienes (n.), parishioners

parten (v.), share

partie (n.), part, portion

passhed (v.), dashed, crushed

patent (n.), patent letter, see N. Sec. III, l. 72

patrimoigne (n.), church endowment

paye (n.), satisfaction; **to paye,** to his satisfaction

paynym (n.), Saracen

pece (n.), piece

pedlere (n.), pedlar

pees (n.), peace

peire (n.), pair

pelet (n.), a stone ball used as war missile

pens (n.), pence

peny (n.), penny; **peny ale,** see N. Sec. II, l. 220

penyes (n.), pennies

penytancere (n.), confessor

peple (n.), people

perfitly (adv.), perfectly

persone, persoun (n.), parson, parish priest

pertliche, pertly (adv.), clearly, obviously

peyne (n.), pain

peynted (v. past part.), painted

peys (n.), weight

piloure (n.), thief, pillager, despoiler of the dead

piones (n.), see N. Sec. II, l. 312

piries (n.), pear trees

pisseres (n.), soldiers' (slang term)

pitaunce (n.), allowance

pite (n.), pity

pitously (adv.), piteously

pitouslich (adj.), pitiable

plastre (n. and v.), plaster

platte (hir) (v.), threw (herself) flat

plededen (v.), pleaded (a legal case)

plese (v.), please

pleyande (v. pres. part.), playing, making merry

pleyned (v.), complained

plighted, y-plighted (v.), agreed, apprenticed, covenanted

plokked (v.), plucked, took

plomtrees (n.), plum trees

podyng ale (n.), pudding ale, see N. Sec. II, l. 220

poeple (n.), people

poised (v.), weighed

pokkes (n.), small-pox

polles (n.), heads (hence 'crowds')

polsche (v.), polish

ponfolde (n.), pinfold, pound

pople, see 'poeple'

poraille (n.), poor people

possessioneres (n.), see N. Sec. II, l. 144

posternes (n.), postern-gates

potagere (n.), soup maker

potel (n.), a measure of 4 pints

poudres (n.), powders

pouke (n.), devil

Poule (n.), Paul

pounde (n.), pound, pound weight

poure (adj.), poor

pous (n.), pulse

pouste (n.), power

poynt (n.), reason, matter

poyntes (n.), details, particulars

poysye (n.), poetry

preise (v.), value

prelats (n.), prelates

prentis (n.), apprentices

prentishode (n.), apprenticeship

presse (n.), press
prest (n.), priest
prestest (adj.), quickest
preve (v.), prove
prey (v.), pray, prey upon
preyere (n.), prayer
preynte (v.), looked sted-
  fastly, gazed
preyseth (v.), praises
Pridie (n.), Skeat suggests a
  hint at 'prie-dieu' a sort of
  folding stool
priker (n.), horseman
prisoun (n.), prisoner
profered (v.), offered
profetes (n.), prophets
pruyde, pryde (n.), pride
pryed (v.), pried, sought
pryked (v.), spurred
prykked, y-prykked (v.),
  wounded
prys (n.), price, value
pryve (adj.), secret, intimate
pryvely (adv.), secretly
pukked (v.), pushed, en-
  couraged
purfyle (n.), fur-trimming
purs (n.), purse, bag
putten (v.), set
puttes (n.), pits, dungeons
pyke (n.), (pilgrim's) pike-
  staff
pyked (adj.), peaked, see N.
  Sec. IV, l. 169
pykehernois (n.), plunderers
  of armour
pyne (n.), pain, punishment,
  see also N. Sec. II, l. 29
pynne (v.), fasten

quarteroun (n.), quarter

quats (v.), said
quaved (v.), shook
queste (n.), inquest
queynte (v. past. part.),
  killed
queyntise (n.), cunning
quite (v.), repay, redeem
quod (v.), said
quykke (adj.), living; (v.),
  animate, revive
quyte (v.), repay, ransom

radde (v.), advised
radegoundes (n.), running
  sores (especially of the eyes)
ragman (n.), document listing
  names, document with many
  bishops' seals
rakyer (n.), scavenger
ran (v.), ran, hastened
rape (n.), hurry
rapelich, rapely (adv.), swiftly
rappe (v.), hurry; rappe
  down, hurry along
rather (adv.), sooner, more
  quickly; the rather, very
  soon
rathest (adv.), soonest
ratonere (n.), rat-catcher
raughte (v.), seized, obtained
raunceoun (v.), redeem, ransom
ravestow? (v. singular), are
  you mad?
rayes (n.), striped cloths
reccheles (adj.), careless
reccheth (v.), cares
reconforted (v.), comforted
  again
recorde (v.), set down, declare
recovrere (n.), recovery

recreaunt (adj.), recreant, defeated

redde (v.), advised

rede (v.), advise

redes (n.), reeds

redili (adv.), easily

redy (adj.), ready

redyngkyng (n.), horse-boy

regne (v.), reign

regratere (n.), retail-dealer

reherce (v.), repeat

rekenynge (n.), account

rekne (v.), count up, settle accounts

releve (v.), raise up again

religioun (n.), religious orders, religion

religiouse (n.), members of a religious order

relyed (v.), rallied

remenaunt (n.), rest, remainder

rendred (v.), taught

renke (n.), man

renne (v.), run

rennyng (v. pres. part.), running, running a course in the lists

repentedestow the? (v. singular), did you repent?

reproveth (v.), disproves

rerages (n.), arrears, debts

resoun (n.), reason

reule (n.), rule, order

reulen (v.), rule

reume (n.), kingdom, realm

reuthe (n.), pity

reve (v.), take away, deprive

reverence (v.), honour, salute

reves (n.), reeve's, bailiff's, see N. Sec. II, l. 427

rewe (v.), rue, feel sorry

rewet (n.), small trumpet

rewle (n. and v.), rule

rewmes (n.), kingdoms, rheums, catarrhs

ribaude (n.), villain, worthless fellow, sinner

ribaudye (n.), ribaldry

ribibour (n.), a rebeck (fiddle) player

rifled, y-rifled (v.), rifled, burgled

rigge-bon (n.), back-bone's

righte (adj. and adv.), very, same, exactly, just, directly

rightful (adj.), true, righteous

rightwisnesse (n.), righteousness

roberdes knaves (n.), see N. Sec. I, l. 44

roche (n.), rock, and see N. Sec. III, l. 72

Rode (n.), Cross

rolle (v.), register, enrol

rongen (v.), rang

roos (v.), arose

ropere (n.), rope-merchant

rored (v.), groaned

roste (n.), roast meat

rote (n.), root, basis, foundation

rouned (v.), whispered

route (n.), company, crowd

rowed (v.), began to dawn

rowme (v.), roam

roxed (v.), stretched

roynouse (adj.), scabby

rutte (v.), snored

ruwet (n.), small trumpet

ryflynge (n.), rifling, plundering

Ryne (adj.), Rhenish
rype (adj.), ready, ripe

sadder (adv.), steadier, more soundly
salve (n.), ointment, remedy
Sapience (n.), The Book of Wisdom
saut (n.), assault
sauter (n.), psalter
savacioun (n.), salvation
sawes (n.), proverbs, sayings
say (v.), saw
scalles (n.), sores
schete (n.), sheet
schewe (v.), show
schrape (v.), scrape
schrewe (n.), wretch
scole (n.), school, education
scrifte, shrifte (n.), shrift, confession
scrippe (n.), scrip, bag
se, see (n.), sea; (v.), see
secte (n.), following of people, suit of clothes
sede (n.), seed
seel (n.), seal
seet (v.), sat
sege (n.), place
segge (n.), man; (v.), say
seiden (v.), said
seigh, seighe (v.), saw
seighed (v.), sighed
seighen, y-seyen (v.), seen
seised (v.), have been in possession
seith (v.), says
seke (v.), seek
seketh (v. 2nd pl. imper.), seek!
sekenesse (n.), sickness

selde (adv.), seldom
sele (n.), seal
selke (n.), silk
selles (n.), cells
semed (v.), seemed
semivyf (adj.), see N. Sec. III, l. 117
sen (v.), see
sendal (n.), fine silk cloth
serjaunts, see N. Sec. I, l. 129
serke (n.), shirt
Sesar (n.), Caesar
seson (n.), season
sestow? (v.), do you see?
seten (v.), sat
sette (v.), plant, place
settyng (n.), planting
seweth (v.), follows
seyllynge (v. pres. part.), sailing
seyne (v.), said
seyned (v.), signed, made the sign of the Cross
seynt (adj.), holy; (n.), saint
shadweth (v.), throws its shadow
shedyng (n.), shedding, spilling; **for shedyng**, to prevent spilling
shef (n.), sheaf
shene (adj.), beautiful
shente (v.), ruined
shepe (n.), shepherd
shewe (v.), appear, declare, admit
shifte (v.), moved aside
sholde (v.), should, had to
shonye (v.), avoid, shun
shope (v.), dressed, planned, devised
shoures (n.), showers

shroudes (n.), rough clothes

shryve (v.), hear confession, shrive

shul (v.), shall

shuldest (v.), shouldest

shulle (v.), must, shall

shupte (v.), contrived, formed, created

sibbe (adj.), related; (n.), relation

siker (adj.), sure; (adv.), surely

sikerere (adv.), more certainly

sikerly (adv.), certainly, surely

sith (adv.), since, ever since

sithen (adv.), afterwards; (conj.), since

sithes (n.), times

sittende (v. pres. part.), sitting

sitthe (adv.), afterwards

sklayre (n.), veil

sleighte (n.), trick, deceit, cunning

slepe (n.), sleep

slepestow? (v.), are you asleep?

slepying (n.), state of sleep

sleuthe (n.), sloth

slow (v.), slew

slynge (n.), sling

smaughte (v.), smelt

socoure (n.), help

solfe (v.), sing musical notes, sing 'sol-fa'

somer (n.), summer, somer game see N. Sec. II, l. 413

somme (n.), some, sum, total

sondri (adj.), various, separate

sone (adv.), immediately; (n.), son

sonne (n.), sun

sonnest (adv.), soonest

sopere (n.), supper

sore (adv.), sorely, painfully

sori (adj.), wretched

sorwe (n.), sorrow

soth, sothe (n.), truth

sothfastnesse (n.), truth

sothly (adv.), truly

sotil (adj.), cunning, clever

souteres (n.), cobblers

souteresse (n.), woman shoemaker

sovereigne (adj.), supreme; (n.), master, lord

spak (v.), spoke; spak to, bespoke, instructed

spaklich, spakliche (adv.), quickly, sprightly, in a lively manner

spede (v.), succeed, prosper

spedde (v.), hurried

speneth (v.), spends

spere (n.), spear

Spes (n. Latin), Hope

spilleth (v.), ruins, spoils

spilte, y-spilte (v.), wasted

spire (v.), make enquiries after

spores (n.), spurs

spronge (v.), sprung, born

sprynge (n.), rod

spye (n.), scout, spy

spynnestres (n.), female spinners

stalworth (adj.), strong

staves (n.), staves, sticks

stedes (n.), places

stere (v.), stir, move

sterre (n.), star

stole (n.), stool

stonde (v.), stand

stoupe (v.), stoop

Stowve, see N. Sec. II, l. 28

streyte (adv.), strictly
streyves, see N. Sec. I, l. 94
struyeth (v.), destroy
stuwardes (n.), stewards, managers
stuwes (n.), brothels
sue (v.), attend on, follow, pursue
suffre (v.), endure, suffer, allow, be quiet
sugre (n.), sugar
sum, summe (pron.), some
supprioure (n.), sub-prior
suren (v.), give one's promise, give security
surgien (n.), surgeon
sustren (n.), sisters
sute (n.), suit, clothing (of human flesh)
suwed (v.), pursued
suweth (v.), follows
swelte (v.), die
swere (v.), swear
swete (adj.), sweet
swevene (n.), dream
sweyved (v.), rippled
swithe (adv.), quickly, very
swonken (v.), worked
swowe (v.), swoon, faint
swowned (v.), fainted, dozed
swynke (v.), work
syb (adj.), related
sydder (adj.), lower, longer
syde (n.), side
syke (adj.), sick; (n.), sick people
syked (v.), sighed
syker (adj.), safer, surer
sylver (n.), silver, money
symonye (n.), simony
syn (adv. and conj.), since

Synay (n.), Sinai
synne (n.), sin
synneles (adj.), innocent
syre (n.), father
sysour (n.), juror
sythes (n.), times
sytten (v.), sit

tabarde (n.), tabard, i.e. sleeveless short coat
tailled, y-tailled (v.), marked on a tally stick; by taille, on a tally stick
taille-end (n.), backside
tailles (n.), tails, roots of trees
tale (n.), tale, account, importance
take (v.), take, lend
taste (v.), feel, dare to attack
tauny (adj.), tawny, orange brown
techen (v.), teach
techeres (n.), teachers
tellen (v.), count
teme (n.), theme, text
temperaltes (n.), temporal possessions
tempred (v. past part.), attuned
tendeden (v.), lit, lighted
tene (v.), annoy, injure
termyned, y-termyned (v.), decided upon, determined
tethe (n.), teeth
thanne (adv.), then
that (conj.), so that; (pron.), that which, those that, who
the (adj.), the; (pron.), thee; (v.), thrive
thei (pron.), they, those
theigh (conj.), although

thennes (adv.), thence

there (adv.), there; (conj.), whereas

there-after (adv.), accordingly

therinne (adv.), therein

there-myde (adv.), with it

there-whiles (adv.), in the meantime

thevelich (adv.), like a thief

thider (adv.), thither

thin (poss. pron.), thy

this (pron.), this, these; **this and that,** the one and the other

tho (adv.), when; (pron.), those

tholed (v.), suffered

thombe (n.), thumb

thorugh, thorughe, thorw (prep.), through

thoughte (v.), thought, it seemed (depending on whether introduced by nominative or dative pronoun), intended to go

thourgh (prep.), through

thow (pron.), thou

thresshewolde (n.), door step

threstes (v. impersonal), thirst afflicts

threttene (adj.), thirteen

thretti, thretty (adj.), thirty

thretynge (n.), threat

threwe (v.), stumbled, fell

thridde (adj.), third

thrungen (v.), thronged

thruste (n.), thirst

tilie (v.), till

tixte (n.), text

to (adv.), too; (prep.), to

to-bolle (adj.), extremely swollen

toft (n.), mound

togidere, togyderes (adv.), together; **they taken hem togyderes,** they go into council

to-helle-ward (adv.), towards Hell

tolde (v.), counted

toke (v.), took, gave

tokenynge (n.), sign, token

to-kirkeward (adv.), towards church

tokne (n.), sign, token

tolled (v.), stretched, were drawn out to

tolleres (n.), toll-collectors

tonge (n.), tongue

torne, tourne (v.), turn

totorne (adj.), greatly torn

toure (n.), tower

travaille (v.), work

tre, tree (n.), tree

tresore (n.), money, treasure

tresoun (n.), treason; **if tresoun ne were,** in peace-time

tretour (n.), traitor

treuthe (n.), truth

trewe (adj.), true

trewes (n.), truce

trewly (adv.), truly

trewthe (n.), truth

triacle (n.), a medical concoction as an antidote against poison

tried (v.), tested

trielich (adv.), excellently

trolled (v.), wandered, walked

tromped (v.), played a trumpet

trufle (n.), trifle, piece of nonsense

tutoure (n.), keeper
tweies (adv.), twice
tweyne (adj.), two
tyen (v.), bind
tyl (conj.), until; (prep.), to, up to
tylye (v.), cultivate
tynkares, tynkeres (n.), tinkers
tynt (v.), lost
tyterers (n.), tattlers, gossips

uch, uche (adj. and pron.), each
uchone (pron.), each one
umwhile (adv.), from time to time
uncristne (n.), heathens
underfonge (v.), received
undernome (v.), rebuked
undernymeth (v.), reproves, rebukes
undertaken (v.), receive, promise
unethe (adv.), scarcely
unhardy (adj.), cowardly
unhende (adj.), ill-mannered; (n.), discourtesy
unite (n.), unity
unjoignen (v.), break, dissolve
unkynde (adj.), unnatural
unlese (v.), open
unlouken (v.), unlock, undo
unpynneth (v.), unbolt
unsowen (v.), unsew, slit open
unspered (v.), unbarred, opened
unthende (adj.), wretchedly small
until (prep.), to

untydy (adj.), crude, unseemly
unyte (n.), unity
up (prep.), upon
upholderes (n.), dealers in second-hand goods, upholsterers
usedestow? (v. singular), did you use?
usurie (n.), usury

vauntewarde (n.), vanguard
veille (n.), watcher
vendage (n.), vintage
venge (v.), avenge
venjaunce (n.), vengeance
venym, venymouste (n.), poison
vernicle (n.), see N. Sec. II, l. 527
vertue (n.), power, virtue

wafrestre (n.), female wafer-seller, see N. Sec. II, l. 582
wage (v.), engage, pay wages
wagged (v.), shook
wake (v.), wake, lie awake
wal (n.), wall
walde (v.), would, wanted
walkene (n.), sky
Walshe (n.), Welshman
waltrot (n.), nonsense, absurdity
wan (v.), gained
wanhope (n.), despair
war, ywar (adj.), cautious, wary
warde (n.), guard
wardes, see N. Sec. I, l. 94
wardeyne (n.), guardian
wardmotes, see N. Sec. I, l. 94
ware (n.), merchandise; (v.), beware

warner (n.), warrener, game-keeper

warpe (v.), uttered

wastel (n.), fine bread

Wastoure (n.), Waster, spend-thrift

watre (n.), water

Watt (n.), (a contraction of) Walter

wayte (v.), watch for, look after

wayved (v.), removed

webbe (n.), cloth (entire piece of cloth of which Eleyne's coat was part); (n.), female weaver

wedde (n.), pledge, security

wede (n.), clothing

weder (n.), weather

wel (adj.), good; (adv.), much

welaway (interj.), alas!

welche (n.), cloth

welthe (n.), wealth, money

wem (n.), stain

wenche (n.), girl, daughter

wende (v.), thought, believed

wenden (v.), make one's way, turn

wene (v.), believe, imagine, think

went (v.), turned aside, made one's way

wepe (v.), weep

wepne (n.), weapon

were (v.), would be

werkis, werkes (n.), deeds

werre (n.), war

werse (adj. or adv.), worse

wery (adj.), weary

wete (n.), wet, wet weather

wete-shoed (adj.), with water in the shoes

wex (v.), grew

wexed (v.), waxed, stopped up with wax

wey (v.), weigh

weye (n.), a particular weight, see N. Sec. II, l. 93; (v.), weigh

weyllowey (n.), woe, alas (hence 'sorrow' in Sec. III, l. 430)

weyghed (v.), weighed

weyves, see N. Sec. I, l. 94

whan (adv.), when

whennes (adv.), whence

where (adv.), where; (conj.), whether

wherforth (adv.), whither

wher-of (adv.), whereby

whete (n.), wheat

whiderward (adv.), in what direction

who-so (pron.), whosoever

whyte (adj.), white

wicche (n.), witch, sorcerer

wighte (n.), creature

wightlich (adv.), quickly

wikke (adj.), wicked

wikkedlich (adv.), wickedly

wille (n.), will; **Wille**, Will(iam)

wilne (v.), wish

wilneth (v.), wishes

wiltow? (v. singular), will you?

wise (n.), manner, way

wispe (n.), wisp, twist of straw, etc.

wisse (v.), teach

wissheden (v.), wished

wist, wiste (v.), knew
wite (v.), knows
with-drowe (v.), withdrew
withewyndes (n.), bind-weed's, convolvulus's
with-halt (v.), withholds
with that (conj), provided that
witnes (n.), witness
witt, witte (n.), mind, knowledge, wisdom, understanding; (v.), blame, see N. Sec. I, l. 179
witterli (adv.), really, truly
wittis (n.), understanding, senses, see N. Sec. I, l. 163
wo (adj.), sad; (n.), trouble
wode (n.), wood
woke (n.), week
wolden, wole (v.), wish, desire, will
wollen (adj.), woollen
wolleward (adj.), with wool next to the skin, see N. Sec. III, l. 204
wollewebsteres (n.), wool weavers
wombe (n.), belly, stomach
wonieth (v.), dwells
wonnen (v.), earn, dwell
wonye (v.), stay, dwell
woon (n.), quantity
worche (v.), work, act
worchyng (v. pres. part.), working
wordyng (v. pres. part.), talking
wortes (n.), vegetables
worth (v.), will become, will be, become; **that thow worth the werse,** lest you should become ill

wote (v.), knows
wownde (v.), injure
wratthe (n.), anger, wrath
wratthed (v.), enraged
wreke (v.), avenge
writte (n.), deed, scripture
wroke (v.), see **wreke**
wroughte (v.), acted, worked, created; **wroughte me to man,** created me as a man
wrynynge (v. pres. part.), wringing (one's hands)
wy (n.), man
wyde (adv.), widely
wydwes (n.), widows
wye (n.), man, creature
wyght (n.), man
wylned (v.), wished, longed
wyn (n.), wine
wynde (n.), wind; (v.), spin
wynkynge (n.), slumber
wynnen (v.), win, regain, earn, prosper
wynnynge (n.), business, success
wys (adj.), wise
wyse (n.), manner, wise people
wyte (v.), defend; **Wyt God,** God defend (us)!
wytte (n.), understanding
wytterly (adv.), certainly
wyven (n.), wives', women's

y-, prefix denoting past participles of verbs (see under main verbal stem)
yaf (v.), gave
yate (n.), gate
ydel (adj.), vain, idle, foolish
ydiote (n.), idiot

ye (particle), yea, yes; (pron.), you

yeden (v.), travelled, went

yeld (v.), repay

yelt (v.), yields

yeme (n.), heed, note

yeode (v.), went

yerdes (n.), yards

yeres, yeris (n.), years

yerne (adv.), anxiously, quickly; (v.), yearn, crave

yete (adv. and conj.), yet

yeve (v.), give

yif (conj.), if; (v.), give

yit (adv.), yet

yive (v.), give

ylike (adj. and prep.), like

ymage (n.), image

ympe (n.), graft, shoot; (v.), graft

ynough (adj.), enough

yonde, yone (adj. and adv.), yonder

yonge (adj.), young

yowre (adj.), your

yowre-selven (pron.), your-selves

ypocrysie (n.), hypocrisy

Yrlonde (n.), Ireland

ysue (n.), issue, offspring

yus (particle), yes

yvel (adj.), wicked, evil, diffi-cult; (adv.), wickedly, with difficulty

yveles (n.), diseases

ywar (adj.), wary, watchful

PRINTED IN GREAT BRITAIN BY ROBERT MACLEHOSE AND CO. LTD
THE UNIVERSITY PRESS, GLASGOW